LEADING FOR "WE" IN THE AGE OF "ME"

THE ART
of
EVERY
THING

DR. GARY WADDELL

This book is grounded in my journey to develop a model of artful leadership. Along the way, I share the stories of those who have most influenced me. Some are referenced by name, some by pseudonym and some are anonymous. I offer their stories only as my recollections and memories.

ASIN B089G8BDMC (ebook)
ISBN 9798643607083 (paperback)
Library of Congress Control # 2020911255

artofeverything@garywaddell.org
www.garywaddell.org/art

"Inside you there's an artist you don't know about."
—Rumi

"May your choices reflect your hopes, not your fears."
—Nelson Mandela

ABOUT THE AUTHOR

D r. Gary Waddell's unconventional approach to leadership has helped countless leaders build strong teams and produce results. His work in the education sector has caused student achievement to soar and has closed achievement and opportunity gaps for historically underserved children and youth. He has been recognized with a variety of prestigious state and national awards in the areas of leadership, education, and human rights.

Gary's focus on daring to trust the hearts and wisdom of his teams is a hallmark of his model of artful leadership. He has held posts such as Deputy County Superintendent, Associate Superintendent, Principal, and Counselor as well as serving as a candidate for public office. Gary served as statewide Chair of California's *Curriculum and Instruction Steering Committee* (CISC) and as statewide Arts Committee Chair.

Dr. Waddell holds a Doctorate in Educational Leadership, in addition to an Educational Specialist degree in school administration, a Master of Arts in Education in counseling, and a Bachelor of Arts in drama.

Gary is a former foster parent of adolescents with special needs and is a lifelong advocate for children and youth on the margins. Originally from Asheville, North Carolina, he currently lives in the San Francisco Bay Area.

Your Free Bonus!

As a small token of our *big* thanks for buying this book and building your skill as an artful leader, we'd like to offer you a free bonus gift, *The Art of Everything Workbook*.

This valuable guide is a tool to help you implement the Framework for Artful Leadership. This short guide provides reflection activities that can be done by yourself or with a group.

In this free bonus booklet, you'll find:

- Reflection questions on each of the key guideposts of the model
- A quick asset map to help you assess your strengths in the artful leadership framework
- Some suggested strategies to start building your mastery of the five components of artful leadership

Download your free content at www.garywaddell.org/bonus

(And while you're there, be sure to subscribe
for additional bonus content!)

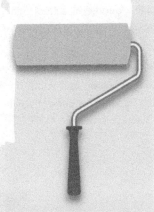

DEDICATION

T his book is dedicated to those leaders who are audacious enough to trust in the power of creativity and connection.

It is for all of those who refuse to color in the lines.
You make our world messy and technicolor-weird — and wonderful.
And we're all better because of it.

Together, may we create a better world one conversation, one connection at a time.

CONTENTS

FOREWARD
BY DEBORAH MEIER

Over the years as a teacher, teacher-director and principal, I've been intrigued by how many teachers do not aspire to become principals. I thought I was the only one. They do not necessarily reject the idea of being leaders, however. Interesting.

They tell me that they love being in the classroom too much to abandon it. Or they love the collegiality that they would lose. Or they imagine it's full of politics and bureaucratic maneuvering that they would hate, not to mention dealing with parents and school boards and the media. I identified with all these arguments, except perhaps dealing with families which I grew to find interesting and satisfying over the years.

But I promised Gary Waddell I'd read his book about leadership in which he describes his experiences over the years as principal and educational leader. I began it hesitantly and skeptically. And as I went from chapter to chapter, I realized I was identifying more and more with his work and his viewpoint.

His path to leadership bridged his experience working in schools with teachers, students, and parents. He learned that the democratic habits of mind and building relationships is essential to leadership. It's not a bureaucratic exercise but is a necessary condition in order to create communities in which democratic work emerges.

Much as I had struggled to simultaneously see myself as the leader (and founder) of a school and a classroom teacher, he had to embrace his background in art and counseling and square that with his leadership.

I had remained a half-time kindergarten teacher in my first role as leader of a small pilot program. I tried doing the same in my second try at Central Park East. By the end of the second year, we all realized this wouldn't do. I became a teacher-director for the next decade balancing my role so that we could continue to see ourselves as a small democracy. Somebody, we decided, had to be free to deal with dissatisfied parents, district staff of all sorts and, of course, the superintendent. When we started Central Park East Secondary school, I had to become a principal. We agreed that I should also have an advisory group of twelve students that met daily for 45-60 minutes and took several trips a year together. It worked. I was lucky to have both a very friendly and clever superintendent who was experienced at giving schools unusual autonomy which made democracy easier.

Yes, in many ways the staff of the school needed to learn to think both as classroom teachers or specialists as well as being the leaders of the school themselves. It challenged us all. Leadership, like democracy, was often messy and required that we bring our various, sometimes conflicting, viewpoints together in our work.

We could have used Waddell's book 35 years ago. But we all became experts at understanding what I had learned, that both advisors and potential dissenters were essential to running democratic schools.

Balancing the role of thinking like both a teacher and a principal became everyone's task. Neither principal Waddell nor I could be as knowledgeable or spend the same amount of time thinking about each role. It required us to trust the hearts and minds of the students, teachers, parent, and communities who cared deeply about our work and what it meant for our students. It's exciting work and is a way of thinking that the leadership of all schools and districts need as well.

Read and imagine yourself in the difficult roles and situations Waddell describes. Whatever your role is, think about how the role of leader helps develop all — be they parents, teachers or students — into stronger citizens of a democracy.

Deborah Meier, June 2020
New York

AUTHOR'S NOTE

In my doctoral work, in the late 1990s, I developed a growing sense that schools served a purpose beyond disseminating knowledge. In truth, I became somewhat obsessed with the notion that they served a larger democratic function and were, in fact, one of the last places in society where we came together across lines of race, class, gender, or any of the other variables that we used to define, categorize, and, too often, separate us. In schools, we came together for a common purpose that was greater than the sum of our collective parts. As I explored this notion more deeply, I found myself inexorably drawn to the writings of Deborah Meier. She did, in very tangible ways, the very things I was contemplating — bringing members of a community together around the shared purpose of creating spaces where students could not only learn but find their voices in a democratic process. If this work was about bringing together those with divergent viewpoints to improve things for our young people, then its standard-bearer was Deborah Meier. I am honored beyond words to have the gift of her reflections on "The Art of Everything" and how its core precepts interface with the notions of democratic schools that empower and engage students and those who care about what is best for them. There could be no more fitting way to launch this work — or one that more humbles me. Thank you, Deborah. Your work has improved the lives of countless generations of young people and those of us who get up every day to try to make their lives better.

Gary Waddell

ABOUT DEBORAH MEIER

Deborah Meier is an American educator, scholar, and leading practitioner of progressive reform within the U.S. public school system. She is the founder of the "small schools movement." Beginning as a kindergarten teacher, Meier helped revitalize public schools in New York City's East Harlem District 4 as founder of Central Park East Elementary School. She helped found the Coalition of Essential Schools, in the 1980s, under the leadership of Ted Sizer. She has received a MacArthur "genius" Award for her work in public education and served as an Urban Fellow at the Annenberg Institute. She is the author of many books and articles, including *The Power of Their Ideas: Lessons for America from a Small School in Harlem*, *In Schools We Trust*, and *These Schools Belong to You and Me*. Deborah has served on the board of FairTest, Save Our Schools, Center for Collaborative Education and the Association for Union Democracy as well as serving on the editorial boards of The Nation, The Harvard Education Letter, and Dissent magazines.

THE ART OF EVERYTHING

This book will save your life.

To be specific, it will save your life of leadership and service. Regarding your broader life, in full disclosure, I hope I'm not bursting your bubble to tell you that your days here are numbered. We're all in that boat with you, so you have some good company.

This book is a guide to finding meaning and purpose in your leadership so that in some way, big or small, you leave a mark that you were here. This book will make your life and leadership count for something bigger.

My own leadership journey has been quite a wild ride with twists and turns along the way. Much of what I learned is about leading (and living) artfully. In its best moments, it has been a pretty damned exciting journey with both spectacular achievements and stunning defeats, and I'm grateful for all of them. In all fairness, I wasn't all that grateful for the defeats in real time — most were actually royal pains in the ass, but as it turns out even those ended up teaching me things that have deepened my leadership.

I have learned much about living and leadership along my journey at the feet of compassion, forgiveness, and humility. I've learned things like the indefatigable nature of connection and collaboration. Mostly, though, I have learned a way of leadership that serves others and contributes, even in some small way, to making the world a better place.

There is an art to this thing called leadership. While it is not the same as the art of the painter or the poet or the dancer, it turns out that it shares much common ground with them. It is an art of grace, and humility, and courage that permeates everything that a leader does. I call it the Art of Everything.

A WORD ABOUT MY JOURNEY

I've spent more than 30 years as a County Deputy and Assistant Superintendent of Schools in California, serving hundreds of thousands of students and as a candidate for public office. I was an elementary school principal in both California and, earlier in my life, in North Carolina, where I also began my career as a counselor. Both of the schools I led cracked the code on closing the achievement gap. We had success improving all students' performance while drastically improving the achievement of historically underserved populations — largely comprised of students of color, students living in poverty, English learners, and students with disabilities.

I have had the honor of serving as a statewide educational leader in California as well as leading statewide committees in the arts. My passion for the art of everything propelled me to learn all I could about leadership and what makes it tick, both formally and informally. Formally, I stayed in school for what seems like a crazy long time, though I was also working in schools through most of it — along the way earning four degrees, including two master's degrees and a doctorate in education.

But here's the thing: I've learned just as much in the trenches, wending my way through the landmines of working in real systems to find a compassionate way to lead people and build shared work that changed the lives of children and the people who served them.

Along the way, I've been humbled to be honored as California's STAR Award recipient in Curriculum & Instruction, recipient of a human rights awards and multiple leadership awards, recognition by local governmental entities for programs that have served children, and, early in my career, as statewide counselor of the year.

Those things have been awesome. But for every acclaim that threatened to make my head too big to fit through the door, there have been times I've been kicked quite soundly in the pants. Those times humbled me and kept me grounded as a learner. In fact, what has mattered most to me, have been the quiet victories that no one has seen — staff members who overcame barriers and excelled with some coaching and support, children whose lives were improved by new programs that mattered in their lives, the daily advocacy for children who would have otherwise been forgotten, and the mentoring of the many leaders in artful and compassionate leadership. Those have been the small victories that made the costs, however high, worthwhile.

Suffice it to say that I have not always gotten it right. In fact, have I had some rather spectacularly stunning defeats. I'll share those, too. This is the sum of what I have learned along the way. This is what I know by heart about leadership as art.

It's worth noting that sometimes learning and self-reflection are a real pain in the ass. They can manifest naturally and easily if you're tuned in to it, but it can also thrust itself upon you, like some annoying house guest who shows up at the most inconvenient time unexpectedly, bags in tow: "Surprise, I'm here!"

In fact, I had that particular kind of uninvited self-reflection recently as I found myself sitting in the late afternoon in the loft of my mother's log cabin, having unexpectedly flown across the country the day prior. I was writing a eulogy for my mother, who had died unexpectedly the day before. This kind, remarkable, and compassionate woman somehow was gone in an instant. How was I to sum up such a life in a couple of pages? What words could capture the grace and breadth of a life well lived, I asked myself, as I fought to keep the reality of the moment at bay for a little while. In the end, I realized that her legacy was about the same principles that guided my leadership journey: compassion, courage, and character.

I wrote in the darkness, the emotions waxing and waning as the night wore on. I wrote of her kindness and courageous goodness. I wrote of the deep wellspring of a mother's love and how those things fed the really quite incredible life I have been blessed to live. I wrote of being the first to attend college in my family. I wrote about what I had learned about leadership — and life — from her simple goodness and grace.

The best leadership, I have found, comes from these places of deep knowing of oneself and connectedness with others. It manifests in that difficult-to-quantify moment that is like some sort of crazy rich stew with equal parts inspiration, persistence, and compassion. It manifests in those unexpected moments that ask us to be open to possibility and to be brave enough to dare something outrageous and bold. It appears in the spark of inspiration and the kind of relentless collaboration that only exists in the space beyond ego.

That, my friends, is the art of leadership, and, it turns out, of life to boot.

It is the art of everything.

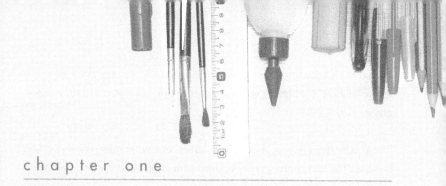

chapter one

GREAT LEADERS... AND THE OTHER ONES, TOO

When I was a kid, there was this Saturday afternoon that I was doing a craft project I had found in a book. I was especially good at following instructions to the letter, so I had gathered all of my materials and laid them out before me on the kitchen table. I was ready to roll up my sleeves and get to work when I did a final check of my items and compared it to the list in the book, I was missing the final item that instructions said was essential. I couldn't find it anywhere. I checked the garage and in kitchen drawers. Nothing. Nada. In a panic and eager to get started on the project, I ran to my parents in the other room.

"Where do we keep the elbow grease?" I implored. "I can't find it anywhere!"

They looked up from what they were doing, confusion giving way to barely contained laughter.

"What?" I said with some exasperation, holding up the book to show them. "It says right here I will need plenty of elbow grease. Do we have any or not?!"

There are days when a leader wishes elbow grease came bottled because the fact of the matter is that leadership is hard work, and there are no shortcuts.

I used to think that really great leaders were kind of like, I don't know, blue moons, winning lottery tickets, or once in a generation eclipses — amazing when they occur, but rare and random. I have learned, though, that what makes those leaders so good isn't some particular DNA combination that they were lucky to be born with. It is a particular cocktail of skills, ways of being, and habits.

We've all been inspired by notable leaders, the superstars on the public stage, people like a Barack Obama, Steve Jobs, Oprah Winfrey, or Cesar Chavez. But there are also quite remarkable leaders who change things for the better in less visible, though equally important ways - the highly ethical local governmental leader, the visionary and bold leader of a start-up, or the committed and relentless leader of a non-profit serving those otherwise forgotten.

All leaders, big and small, share a kind of focused vision that drives them in equal measure with their innate understanding of people and how to motivate and inspire them to step up and do work that shakes things up.

Some of the very best leaders are the leadership corollary of what, in the psychological world, Carl Jung called "wounded healers." They lead from a place of reflection and knowing that usually comes from having had had their share of ass-kickings and royal screw-ups. What sets them apart is their capacity to reflect and learn from these things. They know, or soon learn, that the business of leadership is a humble enterprise that is, at its heart of hearts, all about people.

As it happens, the way of the artist is a lot like the way of the leader. In fact, when you approach life and leadership in the same way that we approach good art making, exciting things can occur. Molding systems and engaging others the way that the artist creates through a blend of skill, design, and creativity opens space for innovative leadership to emerge, the kind of leadership that we all clamor for. You know the kind - those leaders you get excited to work for. I have had the good fortune to work for a number of them throughout my career — they were all leaders who had a vision of service that invoked some greater purpose, who encouraged their employees to playfully innovate, and who had some kind of crazy relentless creativity that kept the whispering voices of smallness, blind adherence to procedure, and "CYA" mentalities at bay.

I hope you've had a chance to work for a leader like that — doing so is heady and inspiring stuff. I'm willing to bet you've worked for the other kind, too. Frankly, I learned as much from them as I did from the good ones — about the things not to ever do. They are the leaders whose approach ranges somewhere between scorched earth — burn it all to the ground in service of stability and order — to random chaos and blatant self-interest and playing their own version of employee Whack-a-Mole with reprimands, tantrums, and unreasonable demands. I never really got these people or how they ended up in leadership positions. Their employees often smile blankly at them, all the while thinking "What's your damage" before hurrying to lunch breaks to fill out job applications.

Too often our experiences have been with the wrong kind of leader — all micro-managey, command and controlley, and tone-deaf leaders for whom we not only wouldn't walk through fire, but would just as soon leave to the battle the fires du jour on their own (or sometimes roast in them). These are the leaders who seem to always be there to step up when there is acclaim to be received, but are quick to point fingers when things go wrong. These are small leaders. Inconsequential. Petty. And, sadly, far too common.

They represent a paradigm of leadership that is deeply baked into the traditional American zeitgeist - and it is a model whose time has passed. It all honesty, I'm not sure its time was ever here, but it was more accepted before we got all inspired and focused on things like agency, equity, and collaboration. Darn those pesky ethics!

I get it. There are times, as a leader, when it's necessary to be courageous and loud, unwavering and resolute. Those traits are necessary, in fact, at times such as the culmination of a project that has been co-constructed with multiple perspectives that have been thoughtfully considered. We all want a leader who will stand up for the right work that we have all built together when the gremlins and naysayers come to tear it apart. But my point is that it is far too common for bombastic and "damn the torpedoes" stances to be mistaken for leadership when they are really just bluster, the art of some deal with the devil, or other BS that has presents itself as leadership. That is the great tragedy of leadership in America. But there is hope.

We have all seen leaders, up close or from afar, who are inspiring and impactful and for whom we would walk through fire. They are the leaders who lead their teams to do things no one thought possible. It's pretty heady stuff to work for one of those leaders and see that person in action.

In my work with quite literally hundreds of leaders over the years, I have seen the skills that high impact leaders exhibit. Not every leader emerges from the proverbial box shiny and with a knack and instinct for inspiring others. On the contrary, most great leaders learn a unique set of skills and attributes that can be cultivated, practiced, and mastered.

Leaders have a thousand things flying at them every day. Each and every one is the most important thing ever in the world and must be dealt with *right now* — or so it feels. For example, a school principal's day is a perfect storm. There are angry parents calling about what a teacher said about their child on a report card or who assigned an unreasonable grade. There are office referrals for kids who told their teachers where they could stick it; there is morning bus duty, lice checks, lunch duty (a particularly inglorious task), meetings to develop individualized special education programs, calls from the district office on where that report is that was due last Tuesday, a team of teachers who want to meet about their desperate need for funding for new materials, and the team from the PTA who needs your ear for just a few minutes to plan the Spring Fling.

Then there are teacher observations and evaluations and, oh yes, making daily rounds to each classroom to check in to be a good instructional leader. That is not to mention playground duty, fire drills, principals' meetings, writing school newsletters, planning staff meetings and professional development, and about a bazillion other things that all must be dealt with — right now. While you're at it, do it all calmly, professionally, and sensitively or the task you just checked off the list has turned into a series of new priorities and deliverables for damage control.

In moments of craziness, when the incoming shrapnel is headed straight for a leader, she has to learn the Great Balancing Act of triage and doing the things that matter first, while keeping one eye ever trained on the end game, their North Star, their "why." When leaders let their eyes drift off of that proverbial ball, there is a nasty bruise coming when that ball smacks them on their ass.

The leader has to steer the ship and keep things moving forward. I once saw an apt depiction of this in a drawing of a large group of people. They were packed in and moving en masse across a landscape, their movement creating a billowing cloud of dust around them. The leader's job is to hold her head above all that fray — to key an eye peeled on where they are moving and make course corrections. That's not always easy. Many times it's damned near impossible, but without leaders who attend to direction setting, systems become unmoored and go adrift.

Good leaders make things better. They build people up. They create new systems that serve some greater good. They are inspiring, and often fun, to work for. They make things better.

So, if you're going to lead, be one of those. Don't be one of the assholes if you can help it. And if you can't help it, maybe consider a profession that has less to do with other living people like, I don't know, being a beekeeper, or a wilderness explorer, or maybe explore something at the DMV?

Good leaders change things. We desperately need more of them. We need more people like you, in fact, who spend the time energy to get better by doing things like reading this book and reflecting on what it means for your own practice of leadership. Good leadership matters. In fact, it matters more than ever in our increasingly divided and divisive world.

It doesn't take much effort to find examples of leaders who are uber focused on the "Me" of leadership. That is, they have a steady eye always trained on their own best interest, political advantage, or bottom line. Good work, if they do it, happens only when it happens to align with their core motivation that revolves around self.

Leaders who begin from a "We" orientation, however, are primarily concerned about outcomes for others. They skillfully build teams, grow their capacity, and engage their creativity. They have a clear purpose, or "why," driving their work and they understand that the success of the organization is also their success. They and their teams sink or swim together.

It is only too easy to find plentiful examples of those leading from a "Me" orientation on the local and national stages. However, powerful leadership that changes systems, innovates boldly, and builds community is firmly grounded in the "We." This book provides guideposts for your journey to the kind of artful leadership that is defined by wisdom, humility, and the shared purpose of "We."

Leadership, done well, may look effortless from the outside, but I'm here to tell you, it's not. It takes some intelligence, a strong sense of self, and more than a little grit to do well.

And it's worth every bit of it.

HERE WE GO

Leadership is way more about communication and collaboration than command and control. It is more about inquiry than edict. I love it and its crazy capacity to foment change, mostly because I think there is a lot that needs changing in our world. They say that the only person who likes change is a wet baby and maybe that's true, but good leaders help people see possibility, opportunity, and hope.

Good leadership is a calling. Without it, good things only happen by accident, a formula that doesn't have much shelf life. Good leaders, though, create the conditions in which inspiring, and sometimes even remarkable, things happen. They don't get it right always, of course, but like any good gardener they keep tilling the soil, planting new seedlings, and applying just enough water until something good takes root. Then they get out of the way and let the magic happen.

It's worth mentioning that while this is a book about lessons for leadership, I have found that its lessons also often hold true for life beyond leadership. You really can't separate the way you live your life and how you treat other people from the way you lead. Leadership is life. Mine. Yours. The lady in the floral housecoat with the wild mane of hair that was in front of me at the convenience store the other morning who was yelling at a display of lighters at the top of her lungs. I couldn't help but wonder what those lighters ever did to her. I bet there was a story there.

Like her, we all have our stories that drive and define us, wise us up, and temper us. Sometimes, no one else understands them so we have to just keep moving forward — and now and again, scream at some lighters because sometimes, too, our stories can break us and we have to start over and move our playing pieces back to square one.

My leadership journey has been about learning to transform environments from ones in which people merely work, to ones in which people ignite in their passions and innovate relentlessly in the service of something bigger than themselves.

That, as they say, is the ballgame.

I love leadership — even with all of its sometimes nutty, sometimes gritty reality and endless demand for elbow grease. I love its occasional triumphs and even the other parts, too. There is a special kind of magic that happens when you bring the right people together around a worthy purpose and guide them to the work, helping them learn to trust themselves, and each other, along the way.

If you do that, you will be a leader — maybe even one of the great ones.

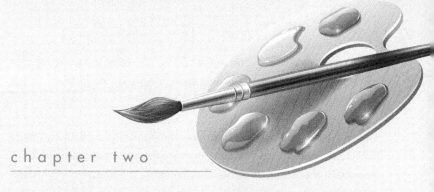

chapter two

A FRAMEWORK FOR ARTFUL LEADERSHIP

My dad was a gruff, no-nonsense old cuss. Don't get me wrong. He was a good man — responsible, courageous, with an infectious, if sometimes biting, sense of humor.

I remember him opening his wallet one day when I was little and handing me a $2 bill. "Put that in the back of your wallet," my dad said, "and you will never be broke." I thought that was funny — and kind of wise — in my preteen view of the world. In the ensuing years, there was something comforting about knowing that $2 bill was in my wallet. I still have it. I suppose it reminded me that my dad's wisdom was there with me, too.

My dad was a fire department chief, a leader who stood up for the people who worked for him. Many were the stories of him taking unpopular stands for his employees. I remember as a kid that he took all the crappy shifts like Christmas Eve and Christmas day so that his staff could be home with their families. For my part, I just wanted him to be home, but over the years I came to understand what an ethic of service and leadership meant. I learned that from his example.

To this day, I have that $2 bill in the back of my wallet to remind me that leadership is service, whether you are leading a fire department or the State Department.

The path of the artful leader meanders through some particularly gnarly thickets. Along this path, though, there are five clear guideposts that can help direct your steps. Together, they comprise the framework for Artful Leadership.

Aspiring leaders often come to me, wanting to know the tricks of the trade, how to better assert command and control, and get people to implement their great ideas. In fact, leadership isn't much about that at all. They sometimes look at me with blank eyes when I say so.

I tell them that leadership is an art form of humility, humanity, and empathy. It is about serving others. It's about producing equitable and ethical outcomes and countering historic narratives that marginalize.

Coincidentally, leadership isn't much at all about how smart you are (although I'm sure you are very, very smart). And, while being smart will help you, artful leadership requires more than just a high IQ; it is strategic and is grounded in the lived experience of those it is designed to impact.

At this point, some of the novice leaders I work with think they have wound up in the wrong conversation. Wasn't this about how to be a leader? They check their phones for confirmation. Or some just text their significant others about this not being what they expected...or what they're having for dinner.

In time, however, they come back to our conversation and set aside some of the notions that they brought in the door about leadership. Then we begin to really talk about a kind of leadership that is grounded in the skills and mindset of the artist — creativity, reflection, innovation: artful leadership.

These components serve as guideposts along this journey towards leadership that builds resilient teams that move systems and ignite change. They represent areas that the wise leader attends to. They frame how the mindset of the artist can bring these parts together into a whole that is greater than the sum of its parts.

These key areas are more lenses than check boxes; more frames of mind than procedures. They have relevance and applicability to a wide variety of leadership styles and contexts. Some are habits of the mind, some are ways of being, and others are skills to master. Taken together, they comprise the Artful Leadership Framework (Figure 1.1) with each component providing a potential entry point into the work of the leader.

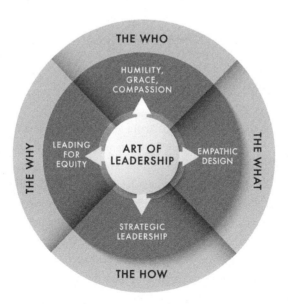

Figure 1.1. Artful Leadership Framework

The components of artful leadership are fluid and dynamic and work in concert to provide a foundation for artful practice. Let's go over them one by one.

The WHAT: Empathic Design

Coming to leadership with an empathic mindset is powerful. Understanding another's experience, what it is like to walk in that person's shoes, and his or her unique challenges and opportunities humanizes leadership. It a way of being that opens doors to thoughtful planning and design.

What do stakeholders think and feel about the problem or challenge at hand? Maybe it is a need for a new registration system for events, or a revolutionary new product, or maybe an initiative that will customize learning. Whatever the need is, this component is about collaborative, democratic, and inclusive design processes.

The WHY: Leading for Equity

Equity is the why of leadership. Artful leadership isn't just a skill set to get things done; it is about shifting systems in ways that make people's lives better. If you work in schools, your work is already deeply grounded in the moral purpose around addressing historic inequities in access and opportunity. If you work in the corporate world, government, or tech sector, finding a why that serves a larger purpose than the bottom line is not only good and ethical practice, it provides a focus and moral imperative for your work. It energizes you; it is good for your soul. What's more, I have learned that soulful work that makes a difference in people's lives is always good business.

The HOW: Strategic Leadership

I just love it when a plan comes together — when the last piece of the puzzle fits in, when the treadmill is assembled, and there isn't a handful of leftover nuts and bolts after the final piece is added. It is great when a new system is ready to begin working. There is a playful sense of enthusiasm that jazzes me when I'm planning the design or implementation of a project. I love that stuff.

Strategic leaders learn to make intentional moves that shift systems. They employ that old Stephen Covey principle of beginning with the end in mind. They know where the heck they are going before they take off, and they have an innate understanding of the levers that move systems.

The WHO: Humility, Grace, and Compassion

Bear with me here. The traits of humility, grace, and compassion may seem more like attributes to develop at the ashram than the conference room. To that, I must say, with all due kindness and deference: hogwash. If there is one lesson that I have learned repeatedly it is that those seemingly "soft skills" are the make or break factors in leaders. Sure they aren't that helpful until married with other leadership skills, but their absence is a deal breaker. Without them, the most skillful leader is little more than a machine getting things done.

The artful leader understands the inherent humanity of leadership. I would go so far as to say that without humility, grace, and compassion, whatever you do as a leader is moot. These traits separate the mediocre, ineffective, or overbearing leader from the one who guides and transforms systems in ways that build people up, expands their capacities, and grounds their work in possibility and promise.

The four components the framework for artful leadership will be your guideposts along the sometimes twisting path toward truly artful and impactful leadership. They are at once simple and complex — simple in their straight-forwardness and yet complex in implementation in real-life systems with competing demands. While their relative importance will wax and wane depending on the challenge at hand, each is an essential touchpoint for the artful leader.

As you reflect on your own practice in relation to the five core components of the Frame for Artful Leadership, you can download a free Art of Everything Workbook that includes reflection questions, a quick asset map, and a few suggested strategies to get you started. You can download the free workbook at www.garywaddell.org/bonus.

And now, let's get started with the very heart and soul of the model — art!

chapter three

THE ART OF
THE MATTER

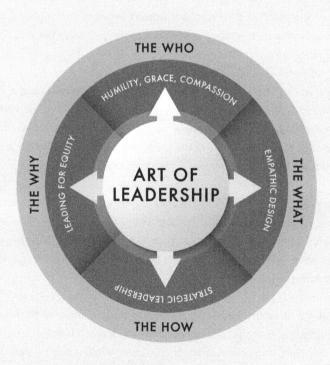

Figure 2.1, The Art of Leadership

A s a novice leader, I didn't come out of the proverbial box with a framework for artful leadership. In fact, quite to the contrary, I came filled with a predictable and dusty collection of leadership stereotypes. Good leaders, I thought, were hardline, bold, and unabashed decision-makers who took no prisoners when they rode in to save the day.

Holy moly, did I have a lot to learn. Thankfully (mostly for those I led back in those days) my lessons were to come quickly.

I had been trained as a counselor and had a very successful practice before I shifted into the leadership ranks. I soon discovered that the things that I knew about people and relationships from were even more relevant in the leadership sphere. Shut the front door! It turns out that those "soft skills" of the counselor weren't liabilities to overcome; they were assets to be leveraged and would come to change the way that I understood the role of the leader.

In fact, when I let go of some of those archaic mental models and leaned into my natural inclination to listen, understand the other's point of view, and collaborate, it changed everything. It is a lesson that I have mentored countless leaders in over the years since: guiding novice leaders to understand that the most powerful leader is often the most humble one.

At the very heart of all the framework for leadership is the "Art "of the model. This is an art that refers to both skillful leadership as well as leading with the mindset of an artist; that is, being creative, reflective, and imaginative. Leaders who approach their work as an artist frame their work differently.

Traditional Western leadership training is more commonly associated with scientific, management approaches. You know the drill — quantify, analyze, plan, implement, monitor, evaluate. While none of these are bad in the proper context (in fact, they are often necessary), they are not enough for leaders who aspire to transform systems and inspire teams.

This approach to leadership has deep roots in Western cultural and organizational management traditions. In the late 19th and early 20th century, a notion of scientific management emerged that would come to extend its tentacles deep into the leadership zeitgeist for decades. Its imprint, in fact, can still be seen to this day.

The theory of scientific management maintained that there is a best method of conducting tasks that yields maximum efficiency. By studying the most effective, high-producing workers on an assembly line in a factory, for example, the manager could develop a process on which to train, monitor, and mold other workers for maximum efficiency.

This notion of the manager's function being one of training and monitoring performance for maximum efficiency became deeply ingrained in our collective notions of leadership. Many evaluation and training systems emerged from this notion of eliminating individuality and variance in the interest of maximum productivity.

These factory models of efficiency shifted over into other types of leadership. Franklin Bobbitt took the approaches of scientific management from the factory into the social sector. Bobbitt worked in the context of curriculum development. Learning, in this context, was broken down into discrete tasks that educators delivered to ensure that the children in their charge attained the target objectives.

This approach was part of a larger movement in the early 20th century that was called the social efficiency movement, hedging predictable routines against the fear of unfettered political disruption and societal chaos. While quantifying and segmenting social systems and controlling for

maximum worker efficiency may have controlled for chaos and individu-
alization, it simultaneously neutralized creativity, innovation, and passion.

These notions extended far into the 20th century. I remember evaluating
teachers in my early days as a school administrator. I assessed their skills,
gauged student response rates, and ferreted out the structures of specific lesson designs. It was all very analytical and rational — and missed
much of what is most essential in good teaching.

What I learned as I got more experience under my belt, though, was that
the amazing work that was happening for kids was happening outside
of the context of these check boxes. I realized that experienced teachers were planning lessons for observations that jumped through these
hoops, only to return to their authentic work with students after I was
gone.

When I began to realize what was happening, I began to tell my teachers
that I didn't want to see an artificial lesson that checked off all of the
boxes that they had designed solely for me to come in and evaluate; I
wanted to see their true interaction and daily practice with their students.
They looked at me with a mixture of disbelief and doubt. I know they
wondered, "What is this guy up to?" After a few observations and some
authentic conversations about teaching and learning that were more
coaching than checkboxes, suddenly our conversations shifted. Teachers
were no longer doing good work with students on the DL but were open
about their successes as well as their struggles and grateful to have a
thought partner in the mission of getting better.

The impact of these 19th and early 20th century notions on leadership that
persists even today. What is clear is that today's leader — who work is
grounded in connection, collaboration, and inspiration — requires a new
framework for leadership.

Today's powerful leadership has very little to do with these traditions. So here's the thing — if you are in a leadership role, or aspire to be in one, you will be doing challenging, often thankless, work. You will see the best of people, but you will also see the worst of them. You will have successes — and you will most certainly have failures. The rewards for the successes will largely be passed along to your team while the failures, yours and theirs, will rest squarely at your doorstep. It is important work that can be invigorating but is also often frustrating and difficult.

Given all of this, I hope that you will aspire to more than merely implementing efficiency. What new things will you inspire? What systems will you co-construct that will alter the course of people's lives? How will you draw out the best in each of your team members to create something that didn't exist before?

I often start each new year with teams that I am leading with the simple challenge that our team has an opportunity in this specific moment in time with its unique set of variables that will never occur in this particular configuration again. It is an opportunity that, once gone, cannot be retrieved. You see, that promise of that moment is about more than efficiency, but it is about leveraging the very best imagination, ingenuity, and passion in ways that change things for the better.

"At the end," I ask them, "when we look back, what difference will we have made?"

chapter four

BLUE DOGS

When we were children, my grandmother took my sister and me to a pottery studio. It was her thing, and I suspect that we tagged along that day as much out of a need for a babysitter as a desire to explore our innate artistry. Nevertheless, she bought us each a plain white ceramic dog figure from the shelves of white, ghost-like figurines, vases, cups, and plates, and we spent the afternoon painting them. My sister, who had an artistic touch, painstakingly detailed her dog, shading Fido's coat with shades of browns and blacks, and detailing the eyes. It was truly a work of art.

I remember excitedly setting mine up on the counter for my grandmother and her friends at the shop to see at the end of the day. I can only explain my dog by saying that it was an explosion of blue. Taking her at her word when she told us to paint them however we wanted to, I remember feeling excited to make a dog that was all my own, my very own, very blue dog. I remember my grandmother's slightly confused stare.

"Well...hmmm. But...dogs aren't blue," she muttered quizzically, almost to herself.

"This one is!" I beamed. I was damned proud of that very, very blue dog.

Maybe you're an artist, or maybe not. Maybe you are inspired by classic portraiture, post-modern installation pieces, stark performance art, or the graffiti-inspired work of a Banksy; maybe not. Maybe none of these are you, but a symphony, hip hop beat, or poetry slam is your groove. Are you a color-in the lines kind of person or does seeing things differently get you going?

What artistic forms excite your soul and invite you to create something new? I bet somewhere tucked away in you lies the spark of creativity of the artist. Hold onto that for a minute, we will come back to it.

I have a good friend, Avi, who is a painter. I am fascinated by his process. It is messy, sort of like an ever-winding road, and kind of brilliant. He has a studio, which is really just a corner of the garage, but he has filled it with his inspiration pieces — a ragtag assortment of sculptures, sketches, paintings, and funky light fixtures. There is a small statue of a ballerina in a Swan Lake-type pose, a troll doll in a tie-dye dress, a sketch of Marilyn Monroe with tattoos, a sculptural piece of an open hand, and a mirrored skull. These things, and many more, exist in this studio space with an old wooden worktable. Its surface is worn smooth by time, its face is a swirling rainbow of colors from the random drops of paint it has collected over the years. It is truly an artist's space: wild, irreverent, and free. Great things come out of there.

My artist friend likes to incorporate "found" items into his art. Watching his process intrigues me. What starts out as a simple idea morphs and changes over and again; then it gets recreated, painted over, and changed until something in it says to him, "This is right. It's done." Before that is a messy, sometimes manic phase of exploration, creation, abandonment, revision, and experimentation. Sometimes he will work a piece for months — using paint and glitter on some object he found on the side of the road or at a garage sale. There are mannequin legs mounted to a square with a wire mesh skirt and a rainbow of seemingly random colors. There is a canvas adorned with a collection of paint brushes, broken plates, and tiles. You name it, it is there. His work is raw, visceral, and sometimes makes you scratch your chin, tilt your head, and say, "Hmmm."

I like that.

Leadership is like that. It is raw and messy and ever a work in progress. The best initiatives often begin with the germ of an idea, a spark of brilliance. For that spark to grow it needs an environment conducive to playful experimentation and creativity. It thrives in an environment that has this as an ethic, "Well, we gave that one a try and it wasn't quite it... we can tinker with it, rebuild it, or start again from whole cloth and we'll have a better solution for having failed this time." Those failures, those successive approximations, are a necessary condition for durable and responsive solutions to occur.

The opposite of them, and the death knell to innovation and inspiration, are environments governed by fear of failure, reward and punishment mentalities, and a range of possibilities that are limited by the parameters of the proven. There are far too many leaders who operate in, and perpetuate, those systems. To break through those environments, or to break out of them when they won't change, requires courage.

When leaders co-create their work, tinker, design, and frame missteps and mistakes as necessary along the road to the final destination, great things can happen. It sometimes takes cojones to stay grounded in that mindset.

If you're like me, you are wired to control all of the variables to ensure that things don't go sideways. But I've learned that I have to let go of all of that and trust the process — which means also accepting that things will sometimes go all to hell. It means accepting that the best results often come after some quite extraordinarily impressive screw-ups. It is a game of control and release and constantly reassessing and judging what things are important to exert control over (things like the law and treating people fairly, and having a standard of excellence and ethics) versus what things to practice intentional release over (things like design, systems, points of view, structures, roles and responsibilities, and so on). It's a dance, to be honest, and when you get it right exciting things can emerge.

So, double down on creative bravery...and embrace your own blue dogs.

chapter five

INNS AND OUTS

E arly in my career, I was invited to participate in a summer institute for counselors. The program placed volunteers in various industries for a couple of weeks to learn about local industries to better guide students on their career paths.

Mostly, though, I was a young professional just starting out and the program paid a summer stipend. So loftier ambitions notwithstanding, I signed up.

I expected a dry and dull couple of weeks in industry. What I got turned out to be a transformative experience that has stayed with me ever since.

On the first day, gathering with my fellow summer stipendees, I surely drew the long straw. I was selected for the "Hospitality Industry" and was assigned to intern in an elegant, historic inn in that was located in Asheville, North Carolina. The Grove Park Inn was built in the early 1900s. It stands to this day as one of the country's most celebrated resorts; a grand, sprawling lodge overlooking the majestic mountains in which it is nestled.

My great-grandfather, in fact, used to tell the tale that when he was a teenager, he and some of his friends found a massive boulder on a mountainside and hauled it via horse drawn cart to the building site of the Grove Park Inn. There, it was used over one of the inn's massive fire-places (and I mean massive — you could easily step inside one of these grand fireplaces). The inn has a storied history, having played host to a stunning array of presidents and governors, actors, writers, and celebrities, along with a steady flow of tourists. They still come there to revel in its grandeur and relax in its setting, perched above the majestic and sweeping vistas of the mountains of Western North Carolina.

In all honesty, I didn't expect to learn much there beyond what types of careers students might aspire to in hospitality — and earn that summer stipend. I learned much more.

What became apparent from the first day was that the inn had a large staff that was focused on one simple concept - excellent service. That meant that regardless whether one was the General Manager, a desk clerk, bellman, or wait person, everyone's job was giving guests an experience second to none. It was the simple principle, but it drove everything they did.

The experience became a formative example of artful leadership and the value of living your values. For example, all staff were trained so that if a guest asked a question out of their area of expertise, rather than telling them whom else they should talk with or giving them directions to an alternate location, they were to stop what they were doing and walk the guest to the proper place. There, they would introduce the guest to an individual who could assist and remain until the guest had received the required assistance.

It was a simple thing that communicated volumes about the inn's priorities and service-orientation. It caused me to reflect on how an organization ensures that its mission permeates all levels of jobs and stands the test of time?

In my observation, it was about their "why." Rather than implementing a sticks and carrots reinforcement schedule related to the practices related to the mission, the organization inspired its staff to understand and own this greater purpose and calling around service. This ethic also permeated the organization's decision-making process.

I learned that the inn had a practice of conducting an annual management retreat to plan for the coming year. What was unique about these events was that a random selection of employees from all levels of the organization were selected to attend with the management team. These employees brought a variety of creative and innovative ideas to bandy about and consider as new practices or initiatives for the organization.

Dynamic organizations bake their values into their very foundations. I've worked in far too many systems that had one set of values listed in a strategic plan but yet practiced quite another set in the daily life of the organization.

MAKING MAGIC

The importance of teams understanding their work in the context of a larger vision is one that you also see in stunning display at the Disney corporation and parks. Inspired by something of a self-confessed passion, I've studied Disney operations and philosophy in some depth and have even had the good fortune to interact with management at a variety of levels of the organization. They have some seminal strategies that they use to conjure up their special brand of magic.

One of the key components is "Traditions," an orientation to the Disney "way" that all new employees, regardless of their level or assignment, take on their first day. The genius of this approach is that this course isn't about how to operate an attraction, clean a guest room, perform on stage, or manage a team. It is about who they are and what they believe as a company — and how that manifests in every task, however small, that they undertake. It frames their "why" as creating happiness.

A friend once recounted a relative's experience with this course. She said that his core job had been in maintenance but that, specifically, he would spend a good chunk of his days with a trusty mop, bucket, and cleaning supplies to be deployed when a child threw up. Now I don't know you, but I'm figuring that neither you nor I would pick this out of a list of jobs that create happiness. Yet he came to view his role as essential to the Disney magic and key to ensuring that guests had a magical experience. He did not focus on the more pedestrian, and decidedly unpleasant, reality of his work. He understood that the "why" of his work transcended the clearly unpleasant "what" of the tasks to which he had been assigned. This approach reveals something about how an organization can simply, but effectively, communicate its core values.

Artful leaders build a shared vision and purpose and put into practice the principles of inclusion, innovation, and shared ownership. Thus, they are inoculated against the dynamic that too often emerges when these are mere buzzwords that appear in a strategic plan.

And yet, as impactful as it is, it takes courage for a leader to genuinely include staff and stakeholders' voices. Many are the novice managers who fear what might happen if they allow this release of control. What will employees say if they are free to speak their minds? What if they raise thorny issues or complain about sacred organizational priorities? What if they ask questions for which there are no easy answers?

The wise leader learns to be a listener, understanding that it isn't about having "the answer," but that the listening is enough. The thing is to facilitate deeper conversation and build shared understanding that is nuanced and emerges only from consideration of multiple perspectives. When that happens, a shared vision can emerge.

chapter six

FINDING YOUR ART

Those is a particularly moving video on the internet of the author Neil Gaiman giving the 2012 commencement address at the University of the Arts. The theme of his speech is "Make Good Art." When life doesn't go as you planned, when things go awry, as they most surely will, then make good art. He eloquently advises his audience of matriculating students to go forth and make amazing and fantastic mistakes and to leave the world more interesting for their being in it. It is good stuff. Wise, simple, and true.

I recently used this concept as the unifying theme for a retreat that I led with my staff. These seasoned educational professionals had gathered to spend a day together in planning and reflection at a local museum. Their day to day work ran the gamut from school district accountability, intervention programs, inclusion support, state standards implementation, to public affairs — not all the most artistic fields, but what they had in common was the artistry with which they each approached their work. It was a powerful day of collaboration, reflection, and art that caused us to think about our work differently and from a more creative space.

There is a simplicity and creativity in art that invites us to engage with each other in deeper forms of connection, collaboration, and imagination.

Art is like air. It is simultaneously everything and nothing. Without it we do not live, and yet it isn't something most of us spend a lot of time thinking about. In fact, most of the stuff that fills up our lives are leaky faucets and washing machines on the fritz, impossible work deadlines, upcoming events with friends, birthday gifts to pick up, trips to plan, health scares, and getting the dog to the vet. You know the drill.

I am willing to bet that you know only too well what I'm talking about. Life gets busy, and there are never enough hours in the day. So, who has time for art? But really, considering the things that matter in the long view of life, who doesn't?

When you read accounts of people who have had near death experiences or who have lost something essential, it is common to hear their very clear and present awareness of how important it is to slow down and appreciate the wonder of life. I recently led a team that had two remarkable women leading it. Within a two-week period, both of them died unexpectedly, leaving their team heartbroken and in shock — and keenly aware of the fleeting nature of this gig we call life. They were there one day and gone the next. There are times in life when everything comes into sharp focus and the things that had seemed so critically important just moments before are somehow trivial and we are reminded anew to spend our time on things that matter.

Leadership, conducted artfully, can be one of those things.

What will you spend your life (and leadership) in service to? Most of the things that consume our time and energy don't seem particularly artistic, creative, or moving. In fact, most are quite resoundingly un-artistic. Yet art resides as much in the "how" and "why" as the "what" of life.

The spark of creativity, the search for balance and grace, the flow that comes with achievement, creation, and innovation permeates everything; it is the essence of art. Art encompasses the creative instinct, the willingness to make something new, and the courage to express a unique point of view — all things that aren't only the stuff of good art-making, but also of good leadership and good living.

Leadership has its own rhythm and artistic sensibilities. Much like any art, it can shake things up and be a force for transformation. It can move us to tears, invoke belly-holding laughter, or cause us to pause and question things. We may love it, hate it, or just be indifferent — often without fully understanding why. It's something we know when we see it, and yet can be hard to define.

What can we learn from the sculptor, the painter, the poet, the dancer, the playwright, the musician that teaches us better how to lead with intention, strategy, and grace? It is in that sacred space between imagination and creation that art exists. It serves as a template for who we are and how we do all that we do — how to do it better, more skillfully, more honestly, and more...artfully.

Leadership is its own art form. It emerges when trust, confidence, and inspiration take root. We have all had moments when just the right team under just the right conditions engaged in acts of spontaneous brilliance. I've learned that that kind of creative flow doesn't occur randomly. It emerges from ways of being and leading that can be cultivated. The techniques and strategies shared here transform outcomes through cultivating a spirit of playful experimentation in which disciplined inquiry occurs.

The creative bent of the artist toward exploration and trial and error that wind ever closer toward a goal, are as powerful in organizational planning as they are in art-making. Now, don't get me wrong, I have seen my artist friends work and rework a piece only to abandon it to the trash heap. Not often, but it has happened, when the art just doesn't work, despite their best efforts.

That happens in leadership, too. Tinkering, empathy, and thoughtful planning will very often get you where you need to be, but not always. Sometimes it's time to let a thing go.

In fact, it turns out, more often than not, that what we create, both in art and in public policy, rarely ends up looking like what we anticipated when we first set out. That is part of the magic of artful leadership.

Art can move us to tears, irritate the hell out of us, or create a sense of tranquility. I dig all that.

I grew up appreciating art. That was an odd thing, really, for a boy from the South whose primary family activity was going to church and whose father's primary interests were ballgames and transistor radios. But I loved words and language, and somewhere along the way, I got a taste for the theatre. I suppose it was a Hail Mary pass from a mother who wanted me involved in social activities and had at long last given up on me with the sports. Doing plays, weekly piano lessons, and writing poetry - those were my secret ninja powers. It would all turn out to be part of my lifelong journey to define who I was on my own terms. It would be a process that I would continue most of my life.

And along the way, I came to love the arts. For me, they transcended the dull and ordinary moments of life. They transported me outside of myself and gave me a window into someone else's life and struggles.

Art, even appreciating art, has always been an active activity for me. Even when I was younger and a student of the theatre and attended a show, I would take "notes" on my program about the production I was seeing, writing feedback to actors and directors whom I would never meet (at least not until my later college days when I tried my hand at directing). I suppose that while I fancied myself a director, those days also trained me to be an engaged and critical consumer of art.

A TWIST IN MY STORY

Then I had a plot twist in my script. Through a series of strategic choices and missed opportunities, I found myself embarking on what would become a career in leadership and education.

I was deeply steeped in the theatre. It was what I knew and what I loved. I had a knack for directing and particularly enjoyed bringing an unexpected vision to a piece. After completing my bachelor's degree in drama, I interviewed for a graduate program in directing at a prestigious school that took one directorial student per year. A friend drove me to the school for my multiple days of interviews, a four-hour trip that was equal parts exhilarating and exhausting. After a grueling series of interviews, performance tasks, and meetings with faculty and grad students alike, I was notified that I was the sole candidate selected for admission in the coming year. I was over the moon.

Now, I had always worked under the assumption that if you do the work, then the universe will unfold to accommodate your vision. Whether it was that belief or just a happily naive sense that if you act "as if" and put yourself out there, then good things happen, I was sure that things would somehow work out.

But sometimes they don't.

This was the first of a number of hard life lessons. Reality hit hard, as it is wont to do, when I discovered that the school was only offering a partial scholarship off its hefty tuition. It was far out of reach for my working-class family. With eyes suddenly open to a harsh reality of the world, I took a deep breath and declined the invitation, every word a painful one to speak. That moment stung, but it also opened doors. This was a theme I would find repeated throughout my life when events would deliver a nasty punch it had been hiding up its proverbial sleeve.

This turning point, however, in time led me to pursue training as a school counselor and, a couple of degrees later, as a school principal — work that I would come to love. Another inflection point for me would come the year when there was a particular confluence of events that led me to make the great trek west to California. I had just turned 40 and something about reaching that milestone caused me to reflect on the meaning of that moment. It was also the year that my father passed away and I was keenly aware that you get one, and only one, shot at life...and you'd best not waste it.

I remember thinking about what I would reflect on about my life when it was at an end. Would I be able to say that I lived it well, that I squeezed every ounce of joy and life out of it, and that I didn't let fear stand in my way?

Moving west was It was a hard decision. I was leading a school that I loved in a district where I had rich opportunities for advancement. I had worked hard to build a high functioning team of really good people who were jazzed about the good things that we were doing for kids. I couldn't have asked for a better gig, except that I in the moment felt the responsibility for both my career and my true and authentic life. So, in my own version of the "Beverly Hillbillies," I loaded up the truck and moved to... San Francisco, never to look back.

It took a unique cocktail of events and experiences that life had in store for me — mixed with a little wisdom, a dose of observation, and a heaping scoop of humility to realize that art was not just a place I had come from. It was something that was in the DNA of who I was as a person and as a leader.

Art, I would learn, could be found in everything. More to the point, everything had its own unique rhythm and art to it, which I would hear when I learned to slow down enough to listen. And so, I did.

And that changed everything.

chapter seven

BESPOKE LEADERSHIP

The other day, I was meeting with a veteran manager, a woman who had a good head — and heart — for the work. She was dealing with some struggles in her department. Her staff were having conflicts and the situation was coming to the point where the wheels were about to come off some major projects. This leader, an out-of-the-box thinker and "doer," was paralyzed by the stress of others' bad behavior. She was struggling to navigate the personalities and daily transactions that she was faced with and it was weighing on her.

As I listened, it was clear that she didn't need me to tell her what to do — or even tell her what I would do in her situation. She needed me to listen, to ask good questions, and to help her find her own answers. She knew what she had to do to get her team refocused positively; she just needed to be reminded of it and empowered to act.

I like the idea of bespoke leadership. It conjures up for me images of a tailor cutting things to size, taking in here, letting out there... letting it out some more there; you get the picture. That is, bespoke leadership is tailored to the unique situation, and people, a leader is faced with. This is a powerful idea. Leadership, at its best, is uniquely tailored to fit the realities of the moment and the needs of your team.

Here's the thing. Everyone has something to say about leadership. Truth is. a lot of it you can tie neatly up and take it out to the trash. While there is a lot of good thinking, research, and reflection on leadership in our collective zeitgeist, there is just as much that is wrong-headed and trivial. So much of the what we read about leadership emerges from the cultural iconography that we have about the leader as the Great Savior, the fearless leader on horseback charging into the fray.

That is a bunch of hogwash. No, really.

The kind of leaders who drive change and don't just process administrivia, understand their leadership as a deeply human endeavor. Look, I'm as big a believer in effectiveness and efficiency as the next guy. I've also learned, though, that while they are good and even necessary, they are insufficient ends for those who step up to lead.

It has been my experience that leadership is some combination of all these things — training, hard-learned lessons, and common sense all mixed up in a cognitive blender and baked over time in the fires of real life with real people in real situations. That is the recipe for good leadership. What sets artful leadership apart in that mix is the humanity, skill, and mindset of the artist-leader.

So, here's the thing. In the end we are all just human and on our own journeys, dealing with whatever unique blend of crazy life has thrown our way — sick parents, acting out kids, health crises, piles of bills, or maybe just a series of really bad hair days. While good leaders bring their humanity to their work, they also know how to metaphorically wipe their feet on the mat, leave life's junk at the door, and get down to work.

It is next to impossible to be fully present for someone as a leader when you're all bogged down in your own stuff. And yet, as irony would have it, the humanity and empathy that come from your own thornier moments of life create the very foundation for artful, empathic leadership.

Now I get that you're probably saying, "Fine, but I'd just as well sail along smoothly and leave the learning to some other guy." I feel you, but life has some shit in store for us both whether we are ready or not. So, my advice is to embrace it and learn from it.

Humble leaders listen more than they talk and guide more than they direct. They are the ones who change things. I can't tell you the times that I have had an issue with an employee that seemed intractable — when they had gotten off-focus, were bent out of shape about something, or were putting up roadblocks, and I sat with them and just listened.

"Tell me what's going on? Help me understand? How can I help?" It's not rocket science, but is simple humanity. Nine times out of ten we got past the boulder that was blocking our path and built some common purpose, respect, and open channels of communication just by listening to one another.

The art of leadership is at once dizzyingly complex and insanely simple. Along my journey towards more artful leadership, I learned some basic principles that are grounded in academic discipline but also are common-sense approaches.

As I've said, artful leading is inseparable from artful living. Those whose lives are petty and mean-spirited will be petty and mean-spirited leaders. They may, at best, become mildly competent managers, but never true leaders. True leaders care about others and what they think and believe. The best leadership resides in the genuine conversation that occurs when leaders refuse to take the easy road of giving directions and instead lean in on the other person's humanity.

There is power in leadership behaviors that are collaborative and facilitative rather than directive and controlling. Don't get me wrong. There are times when what is needed is a directive approach — for example, when a team has engaged in a thoughtful and inclusive process to identify a plan but there are still naysayers who won't get on board. Times like these require resolute action. There are also the inevitable times that test a leader: times when the ethical thing to do isn't easy; when the right course is fraught with peril of one sort of another, yet it is still the correct course to take.

Even these times, however, do not exist in a universe devoid of humanity, humility, or compassion. In fact, I find that the moments when those traits are the most difficult to summon are when they are needed the most.

chapter eight

COURAGEOUS CREATIVITY

I have an odd penchant for new slants on old ideas. Something about taking a dusty old thing and repurposing it jazzes me. You know, like the home renovation shows that reimagine old spaces by highlighting and updating what was there before, rather than merely eliminating and replacing it. I love that. It's a lot like good leadership.

I have a turquoise, distressed hutch in my dining room. It was a passion project (you know the type — when you get in the middle of it and then swear you will never do it again)? But I love it when a boring, traditional piece comes back to life to rather than ending up in the dumpster. The surface is pretty spectacular — the cracks in the turquoise overcoat reveal the black paint underneath. It is just the right mix of modern, old, funky, and artsy to satisfy my palate. It's one of my favorite things.

How many leadership processes are like that — prefaced by planning and preparation but needing also to embrace the messiness of the process until something new emerges?

Creative leadership expands our ways of knowing, deepens our connections, and creates new things that, in large or small ways, improve people's lives. It takes some courage.

There are always those whose voices urge you to settle, to accept the good enough, and to relax into familiar patterns that don't upset the apple cart. It's tempting to succumb to those voices, particularly when leaders don't have a bold, positive vision of the future. The "Collect your check, don't make waves, and let's get out of here at 5:00" mentality can wear you down. I know. Creative leaders have the courage to upend these carts and send the metaphorical apples rolling in every direction. After all, creative leaders are, in essence, just creative people who know how to guide and support others along their journey of fecundity and exploration.

Creativity lives right at the heart of decision-making. It seems somewhat antithetical at first — certainly there are times when full-blown creativity can get you in hot water. In fact, I'd highly recommend reigning in creativity when it comes to budget processes, applying rules and standards fairly, and adhering to legal and ethical parameters. In fact, I advocate being organized, and boring, and predictable in these areas — I mean, really. But transposing that same mentality onto the leadership work of building teams and designing solutions, products, or initiatives, is antithetical to achieving success. Creativity provides the best roadmap for true transformation incorporating skills such as brainstorming, blue-sky thinking, and exploration alternate perspectives around whatever problems of practice are swirling in your morning coffee.

Not infrequently, I have had managers that I supervise come in to meet with me and I can see that *look* in their eyes. Something has gone awry; they have run afoul of some organizational practice; there is a seemingly impossible situation with a staff member, or there is a politically volatile situation brewing (or exploding). It is those moments when I have learned to pause and ask good questions: "Tell me what happened?" "What are you considering?"

Most of those conversations end with a process in place to gather more information, seek input on solutions from those with skin in the game, and to think strategically about how a solution will be implemented. The lion's share of it, though, is about leaning in on creative thinking. It is essential to build those creative muscles in leaders. If you have the right people in leadership positions, they know the right solutions already; they often just need time and space to gather information, ideate, and then build a plan.

Imagination is the heart and soul of the creative process. Paired with skill, self-reflection, and collaboration, it is the secret sauce of the creative. It turns out that those same traits and that same creative, art-making process is also the one that great leaders, educators, and innovators use to excel in their fields.

I love the creative process. There is a feel when you are in the throes of creative flow; when you lose sense of time and become immersed. There is an energy that generates spontaneously when something new take shape — whether that is an idea, a written piece, or consensus at a meeting.

It's infused into everything. It is, in fact, the heart of the art of everything, that artistic sensibility that permeates good art, good public policy, and good leadership. It is a way that we connect and lead. It's the way that we research, innovate, teach, and learn.

Think of a musician riffing, the spontaneous energy that emerges at a poetry slam, the unexpected that emerges in improvisation. None of these things happen by accident — each requires preparation and skill, but also a willingness to put aside the prescribed norms and innovate in the moment. That idea transcends disciplines.

The task of the leader is to push teams to think outside of their traditional norms through structured, facilitated creativity. Content aside, there is value in getting teams thinking differently, be it through arts or consideration of seemingly unrelated, or even divergent, ideas. I have had some more traditional managers ask, when I have planned a retreat or convening leveraging their creative thinking and imagination, "But why don't we just work in teams to get our work done? We have a lot to do and time is at a premium" And I get that. We are all far too busy with more to do than hours in the day to do it. But doing more of what we are already doing by its very definition keep us in the same space and neutralizes innovation.

Getting people out of their day-to-day patterns of thinking (and doing), gaining some fresh perspective, and breathing new life into decision-making can unlock creativity and infuse it with focus and energy.

MANY HANDS

At a recent staff retreat at an art museum, beyond the content that we were working with, the team spent part of the day interacting with the artwork and exploring the differing perspectives through which we experienced them. Creativity and new thinking can reenergize a worn-out team, reminding them of their core purpose and causing them to imagine possibilities rather than merely grasping for easy answers.

One particularly memorable staff retreat was stalled out in the early days of planning. The team was frustrated with planning a division-wide meeting that would engage the management team as well as the administrative support staff. The initial planning team consisted of both administrative assistants and managers. It quickly became apparent that a small group of administrative assistants had enthusiastically inspired with a variety of creativity ideas. We realized the opportunity to leverage the creativity of the assistants and empower them to implement their ideas. We quickly restructured the team, putting the assistants in lead of the team with the managers supporting their work.

The resulting, energetic division-wide meeting helped us all to connect more deeply. Teams wore unique colors to exemplify the cognitive tension between work groups, each with its necessary focus, and the beauty, literally and figuratively, of bringing their "colors" together. Large balls of yarn were tossed around a circle of staff from different departments to make visual the connections between teams. The meeting concluded with a gallery walk of maps that teams had created showing the connections between departments. At the end of the day, teams understood their own work in more nuanced context and connection with their colleagues. This particular activity would not have been on the radar of the initial management design team had the administrative assistants not been given liberty to unleash their creativity and realize their vision.

Recently, I convened a statewide team to provide advice on the design of a leadership tool to support the implementation of statewide academic standards. While not the most joyful or creative content matter on its face, there was great thinking and potential that we could mine if we could engage participants, all experts in their respective areas.

I began the day with them with some background on a design process that we would employ, urging them to trust the process. As these teams would ultimately be offering their guidance on a tool to assist educators in the field, the process began with empathy interviews to better understand the perspective and experience of those who were currently struggling with the implementation of standards in their day to day work.

Beginning with the lived experience of a single user provided us a doorway to more deeply understand the problem at hand with specificity, rather than in generalizations. I asked participants to set aside their clear expertise and professional roles for the morning and only be present as a listener so they would better understand individuals' lived experience. The process relied on — and, in fact, required — this type of deep and intentional listening.

Each small group had one interviewee who had worked with implementing standards from a different role: one was a teacher, another was a principal, another an assistant superintendent of instruction, and yet another a superintendent. The struggles and triumphs that they each recounted shed a unique light on the work at hand. Notably, while these were successful practitioners, none of them had figured this thing out. In fact, they were there to share their successes and *failures* in implementing state standards.

There was an almost palpable sense of "Well... hmmm" in the room before we dove into the work. I urged them again to trust the process and engage as a listener and a learner. There is an engaged and open energy that emerges when one listens deeply to stories. To their credit, these seasoned professionals shifted from being experts with points of view to defend to being listeners seeking only to understand the stories that they were hearing.

The groups discussed what they heard — what their interviewee said, felt, and did. This produced some quite fascinating perspectives on the work. What had been a dry and scholarly discussion turned into a rich one full of meaning. We would very likely have missed much of this depth of understanding had we jumped to "solutionizing," that tendency to rush to fix things before we have truly taken the time to understand them more deeply.

There is wisdom and truth in authentic experience. This kind of creativity activates different spaces in your brain — draws us out of the constrictions of policy and protocol, personality and practice. It lets us, even if for a brief time, imagine "what if."

That is the space where true innovations emerge. And they did. The understandings that the team gained added depth and context to the model that they built together over the course of their work. It was a model that resonated with practitioners having been grounded first in authentic experience rather than theoretical constructs.

LEADING FOR EQUITY

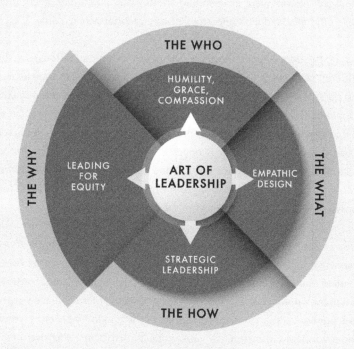

Figure 3.1, Leading for Equity

T he students came to the door of the unused classroom, a room used most often these days for meetings, small group sessions, and storage. Its dingy wood and metal chairs, remnants of another time, stood in a circle, their accompanying desks shoved back out of the way. A few students and parents were in the room already, their affect quiet and guarded. A student approached the door tentatively, a green hall pass in her hand. I greeted her, and she hurriedly found a place in the circle. Over the next few minutes, the twenty-five or so chairs would slowly fill up with students, some sixth graders, and some as young as third grade, amidst a scattering of parents.

The students gathered in the room were unique and remarkable in their own ways. They were boys and girls, budding artists, athletes, and academics. A couple were at ease and chatted and joked with each other while others looked a bit uncertain, unsure of what was to come.

Closing the door, I joined the circle. For all of their myriad differences, the students assembled today had one thing in common: all of the children and parents in the room were African American. They had come to participate in an affinity group about what school was like for them and to share their truth with me, their principal, notably the only white person in the room. This was to be a conversation that would hinge on mutual trust. This was the first such group I had conducted, having heard from both parents and students in one-on-one settings that they didn't feel known, heard, or seen in the school. I wanted to understand.

They weren't here for a lesson, group therapy, or an academic activity. They were here to have an honest conversation about what it was like to be them in our school community. They had each been invited to attend, as had their parents, with the promise that only the themes that emerged from our conversation would be shared, nothing identifiable or personal. Understandably, the parents were initially suspicious and had many questions before they consented. When we spoke, we did so honestly, as they assessed my motives as well as checking in with other African American parent leaders who knew me. They had done their due diligence and now here we were. The time had come.

Our conversation was honest, straightforward, and unflinching. I have never forgotten what I learned in those days. I would later come to lead large projects around equity at the local, county, and state levels and — perhaps as importantly — to advocate for an equity lens in settings where that was not a regular point of conversation. But none of that had transpired yet. Today, I was merely their principal.

I knew going in that this process hinged on our shared trust. These parents and students had every reason to distrust me — while I had worked hard to walk my talk around equity, I was also part of a system that had long disenfranchised them.

I told them that they were free to speak their truth. There would be no office referrals, follow ups, or meetings as a result of our conversation, unless they requested them. This was about dialogue and understanding. I was asking them to trust me enough to share their truth with me so that I could be their advocate in making our school better for them and for us all.

The floodgates opened.

They spoke of being treated as the "other," of being treated as if they were "different.", or somehow "less than." They recounted that their teachers communicated lower expectations of learning for them, as if they were already branded as less capable; yet they faced steeper consequences than the white students when they made mistakes. They spoke of race-based comments on the playground and how their teachers were uncomfortable addressing those. Mostly, they spoke of how uneasy they felt as African American students at our school and how we had collectively made their experience and journey to success much harder than it should have been.

I would later repeat this process with Latinx parents and students, creating a safe space for them to talk — to each other and to me — about what it was like to be them in this place. These were all conversations that I will never forget.

Sometimes to the chagrin of the more traditional teaching staff who preferred a more punitive stance, my approach to the disciplinary role of the principal was heavily influenced by my counseling background. I tended to do more listening than talking, for my goal was getting to the heart of issues and planning strategies together with students as they navigated the day-to-day challenges that school sometimes put in their way.

I've learned that good leaders are good listeners and, more often than not, good people, too. They are, in fact, people who have learned that while they surely have important things to say, putting their own ego on pause for a moment to understand another's point of view changes things. And, sometimes, it changes them, too.

This essential component of the Artful Leadership Framework is about finding your purpose and using that as a yardstick to measure your success. In this section, we will dig deeper into the "why" around equity and the critical role that it plays in leadership.

If you're going to lead, you'd better start with knowing who you are. In fact, even if you're not a leader, I highly recommend knowing yourself. I mean otherwise, if you lose yourself, you won't know who you're looking for.

Quite seriously, though, growing into yourself is an empowering thing. It can take time to find your authentic voice and know what ground you stand on. One of my memorable lessons on this particular content came at the outset of my doctoral program. I was just beginning my studies in an Educational Leadership doctoral program. I felt confidant and self-assured - firm in my sense of right and wrong, good and bad, just and unjust. I was "in the know" and had this education thing figured out. I mean, come on, I had just been accepted to a doctoral program, having already completed three other degrees with years of successful practice in schools behind me.

Dude, I was the guy!

I loaded my syllabus and materials in a big-ass binder (I was to become somewhat famous for my huge binders that I put together for each course, if I do say so myself). Then I trotted myself into the first class — all bright and shiny and self-righteous.

My first course would change all of that and shake my assumptions about just about everything I held dear in education, and, eventually, to find my own voice and the courage to share it. It is a benefit that I never expected, and it made all the difference in my subsequent learning, and leadership, ever since.

My professor at that time was a woman named Penny Smith who would become pivotal not only in my education but also in my understanding about leadership. She was a wise, bitingly intelligent, and keenly observant professor. Penny was to become my dissertation chair and mentor who would push me to think critically, speak my truth, defend my positions, and question everything. For the time being, though, she wasn't any of that — she was just quite quickly becoming a rather annoying fly in my proverbial academic ointment.

Penny is one of those people who, I determined, had some kind of crazy superspy x-ray glasses that sees right through the bullshit, subterfuge, and airs. She was a student of history and, as the semester began, she led my cohort of doctoral students quite deftly through the history of education and leadership. Hers was an unflinching look that considered the tightly woven threads of historical shifts, political and social dynamics, and key inflection points that shaped our shared understanding and social construction of education.

And damned if all of this didn't push my thinking and bump (quite annoyingly) up against my firmly held beliefs about schools and leadership. It was quite unsettling and, if I might say, quite rude of her to mess with my leadership mojo in such a way!

And yet, as it turns out, the bedrock beliefs that I held weren't black and white facts from the Tome of All Knowledge and Wisdom at all. They were simply assumptions and beliefs that had been made by me and others. To realize that was a real kick in the pants! I mean, come on, leave a fella some illusions to hang on to. Yeh, no. That wasn't happening. These revelations would shift and shape how I thought about leadership ever after.

Suddenly, I saw shades of grey everywhere. There are, I realized, a box full of assumptions that people pack up with them in the morning — beliefs about work, assumptions about children and families, values about the role of leaders... you name it. And most of these were held as hard and fast rules, just the way things are.

TRUE NORTH

With my newfound understanding also came a dawning that the work of the leader is about pushing systems, and the people in them, to question these assumptions and contribute to a future marked by more robust, inclusive views of opportunity not just for some or most, but for all.

That is work that is not for the faint of heart. To do it, you had better know who you are and have a firm sense of the ground you stand on. For me, a whole lot of that is wrapped up under the heading we call "equity." While a lot of what I will share is in the context of schools, the conversation is relevant to any context that involves... well...you know, human beings. The big picture here is that equity is all about differences in treatment, opportunity, and experience based on the skin color, zip code, ability, language, LGBTQ+ status — or any of the myriad other ways that we have collectively come to sort and select people.

It is worth noting that historically we haven't always gotten this right. Sure, we've made some progress here and there, but we still live in an America that is wildly different for people of color, for those living in poverty, and immigrants.

Leadership is about creating the conditions for good things to happen. It can do that beautifully or it can be a force that totally screws things up. That means that every leader, at one time or another, has to grapple with what it is that drives him or her. So, here is the thing, we all have a finite amount of time here to do whatever it is that we are going to do — so don't waste it on things that don't matter. Ensuring that the forms are completed properly and that folks comply with the posted signage may have its place, but I want my time to count for something more than that.

I suspect that you do, too.

In his seminal memoir, Man's Search for Meaning, Viktor Frankl recounts his quest to find meaning while in the Nazi death camps. I have always found inspiration in Frankl's words. Even under horrific conditions, he summarizes his observations in a quote from German philosopher Nietzsche, "Those who have a 'why' to live, can bear with almost any 'how'." Frankl concludes that the primary human drive is the pursuit of meaning — a simple, yet profound, reminder for leaders.

At the end of the day, what is your work all about? Whether you know the answer to that question and are merely checking yourself on your assumptions and recalibrating — or if you are a new leader still figuring out your "why," this is where you begin.

When I was just starting out in leadership, it seemed intuitive that my "why" would be pretty straight-forward. Doing good things for kids, right? Boom. Done.

My commitment to children and youth on the margins was well established. I had had the perspective associated with serving as a foster parent for adolescents with special needs. I had worked for years as a counselor, listening to children and youth sort through the ups — and more often downs — of their lives at home and school. But something was missing.

My work took off when I honed my own sense of purpose, advocating for children who were not historically served well by schools. These were the children and youth from whom I would had long heard stories of how schools had failed them. As I shifted into leadership roles, I became aware of the potential for public policy to exacerbate or ameliorate the historic differences in treatment and outcomes for children, youth, and communities, particularly those who have been historically underserved.

This shift from doing good work for individual students to shaping systemic work was a critical one that would influence everything that followed for me. In short order, equity became my "why".

The term "equity" means something different to just about everyone who uses it. Finding its meaning for you — and understanding it may have another meaning for others who have walked a different path from your own — is the first step in embracing equitable leadership, a core condition of artful leadership.

I learned through my experience and the voices of those students and parents who bared their souls with me that what is important is not a student's "A" or "D" work or their studious or rowdy behavior. It is how we see them and respond to them. Do we see them as full of promise and on the cusp of opportunity or as hopeless and annoying? I learned that the answer to that question matters. A lot.

These things will deeply influence how you lead, whether you are leading a Fortune 500 corporation, a small business, a book club, or a swim team at the Boys and Girls Club. Adjust that lens toward equity, and I guarantee that the people whose lives you touch will have a far better chance of achieving success.

chapter ten

WHEN THE BUILDING IS ON FIRE

The room was bustling with nearly 100 principals and district administrators. There was always a buzz at these events — fueled by packed agendas, updates on the priority (or crisis) du jour, and the busy chatter that emerged when people in isolated leadership roles assembled with colleagues fresh from their own trenches to commiserate and plan together.

We were well into the accountability update, receiving site reports and monitoring tools from the district's assessment director, when someone tapped me on the shoulder. I looked up from the data I was buried in. A bespectacled administrative assistant whose name I didn't know handed me a hastily scribbled note.

The note was short and to the point, "Call Jane — emergency."

Now, those are only three simple little words, but they caused me to sit up straight and look at the messenger for more information, her blank stare telling me that all she knew was on that note. The Jane in question was my school secretary, a highly skilled woman who handled the thousand daily demands of her job with aplomb, keeping her cool in the onslaught of reports, phone calls, requests from classrooms, angry parents, students with runny noses, pink eye, not to mention the occasional seagull droppings in hair — a particular hazard of this school near the bay.

Being typically unruffled, Jane's definition of emergency was not a particularly reactive one. In fact, it had just been recently that I had returned from a principals' meeting only to learn that some students had set a trash can on fire after school in the boys' bathroom. Thankfully, the offending blaze was quickly put out and the dispatched fire trucks had verified that all was well. Jane hadn't called me out of the meeting for that — when the building was, quite literally, on fire.

I could hardly imagine what event had prompted this note!

Scrambling out of the principals' meeting and looking for a phone, I called my school, images of plumes of smoke filing my increasingly anxious mind's eye. I reached Jane on the phone, and she began speaking in a flurry of words...

"I'm sorry to call you out of the meeting, but... well, Monique is here." It took me a moment to register what she was saying. Monique was a fifth grade student whose family had moved to another city a few weeks earlier. Had something happened? Had they returned? A million questions raced through my mind, though none of them explained the emergency call.

I had met Monique just a few months earlier, at the beginning of the current school year. She was a fifth grader, although she could easily pass for a student years older. She was an African American young lady with a mane of raven hair and a voice that projected well down corridors and across the school yard. She said little that was not delivered with confidence. Monique had amazing chutzpah and a courage and self-confidence that belied her years. She was on a path to becoming a self-reliant, assertive young woman in the future. For now, however, she was a fifth-grader who was struggling with a system that didn't quite get her.

Some of her teachers did not have such a positive view of Monique's special attributes. When she was matched with the right teacher who engaged with her, knew when to let her fly, and how to help her moderate her very direct approach to whatever problems she encountered, Monique would excel. But any teacher who was looking for quiet compliance that more fully resembled traditional norms of classroom behavior often found themselves at odds with this feisty, self-confident girl.

As a consequence, Monique had become a somewhat frequent visitor to the office. She and I developed a rapport. On more than one occasion, she would just suggest to a teacher with whom she was brewing a conflict to send her to the office. Our conversations would follow a predictable pattern when she showed up with an office referral in hand, often preceded by a phone call from an exasperated teacher.

"Hi, Monique. What's going on?"

She would usually plop down in the chair beside my desk and describe the power struggle of the moment with a heavy sigh of exasperation and the not-infrequent eye rolls. I found that my counseling hat was a more useful to Monique than the traditional school disciplinarian one that she was quite masterful at pushing back against.

To give Monique her due, as she described whatever disagreement had started the incident and how it had escalated, Monique was as quick to adeptly describe her own mistakes as those of her teachers.

I would listen and nod. Before long, I didn't have to ask the next questions. Monique would go ahead and tell me what she could have done to handle the situation differently. I would nod.

"And...?" I would ask.

"And I need to go make it right with her..."

"Okay."

At which point we would problem solve a bit about just what "making it right" would mean in the context of the given situation, and I would talk to the teacher to learn more and to share Monique's restitution plan. Then I'd turn it over to them to work out.

In all fairness, this bold and sometimes brash young lady could be a handful in a classroom 30 students. Yet it only took a bit of humility, genuine interest in her point of view, and patience to redirect her when her temper flared. I would watch in admiration teachers who handled this masterfully and I would watch others, some of them veterans, who would dig in their heels and refuse to bend or make an effort.

"I don't do it for the others, and I won't do it for her," was their mantra. This didn't garner them much success; Monique was all too prepared to stand her ground.

Unbending teachers had missed the critical distinction in their understanding of equity, conflating and confusing it with equality. I got their confusion; it can seem intuitive to think that "fair" means that everyone gets the same thing. Clearly, when we were arguing over the size of a piece of pie with a sibling growing up, no one thought it was fair for their sibling to get the heftier piece.

But, as it turns out, equity in opportunity is not pie. There is not a finite amount to distribute. Children and youth come to the schoolhouse doors with drastically different experiences, opportunities, and resources. To treat each of them the same is inherently inequitable when they are all unique. I learned, somewhere along the way, that all it took was to be able to say to another child, "I know that she is getting something more than you are today, and I promise you that when you need it, I will give it to you as well." Kids get this. It is the adults that too often do not.

"Is Monique there to re-register?" I asked Jane, still confused by the urgency of the call.

"No. Something happened. I'm not sure what. She ran away from home and made her way here — she wants to talk to you. She said she didn't know who else to talk to."

I was silent for a moment. Monique's new home was in an urban, inner city setting that was a good hour or more away from our school site. How this fifth grader found her way there on her own was a testament to her tenacity and ingenuity as well as incredibly frightening when one considered the myriad things that could have gone awry on her solo journey. Asking Jane to give her the phone, I spoke with Monique. She told me of an argument she had had and that she had run away and thought she could talk to me and I would help her know what to do.

I told her I would head back to the school to talk with her more. I told her I was going to let her parents know where she was and ask them to meet us at school where we could all talk this out.

"Thank you," she said, a vulnerability in her voice that she seldom revealed, but that spoke volumes. "I didn't know where else to go."

We all need somewhere to turn when everything goes to pot. That place usually involves someone who cares about us unconditionally and who we know will be there and listen, even if we have screwed up royally.

The fact of the matter was that I really hadn't done anything particularly remarkable with Monique. I had only listened to her, respected her voice, and believed in her capacity to solve her own problems. Turns out, that was unique in her world.

Otherness and *belonging* are social constructs. Consciously or subconsciously, our systems stack the deck, defining "normal" and expected as what success looks like in our dominant cultural context. It is critical that we nurture and develop a diverse work force that consists of those who have walked a different path and who bring a divergent set of experiences to bear.

Never underestimate the power of the simple task of just *listening*. It isn't always easy. Believe me, I know. Most of my professional roles have come pre-packed with more responsibilities and demands than there are hours in the day. These create an environment in which I find myself rushing to put out the fires and continually moving things ever down on my proverbial "to do" list.

It's easy to be distracted from getting to the tasks that are important such as attending to culture, belonging, and equity. It is an intentional act, and sometimes a courageous one, to move those things up on "the list." It is not easy to pause in the mad pace of things to stop and listen to a child, or a parent, or a staff member who is feeling slighted, misunderstood, or at a loss. These moments, however, are well spent in deep listening and in humanity. They can save not only your school or business, but it is not overstating the case to say that they can make the difference in someone's life.

As for Monique, we had a long chat and processed the turbulent events that had led her to my office that day. Her parents soon arrived, as I had called them to let them know she was okay. And she was. In fact, she was a little better equipped and empowered than she had been the day before, knowing that there were still people who cared about her and would be there for her when the chips were down.

chapter eleven

OUR MOONSHOT

J ose sat in his 8th grade science classroom quietly staring at his
book, the jumble of words there a mystery to him. The bell rang, its
harsh sound echoing through the tile hallways. Jose released the
breath that he was holding out of fear of being called on. He picked up
his books and came to the counseling office down the hall.

I had met Jose when he had registered, just a month prior. His family
had made the not insignificant trek from Mexico to North Carolina. His
mother would tell me that they wanted a better future for Jose and his
young twin brothers. For Jose, the reality of the road to that future was
a treacherous one.

He spoke conversational English with hesitant fluency. However, it soon
became apparent that his written language was sorely lacking as was his
academic foundation. As his 8th grade counselor, I saw him struggling
and scheduled him into an "Office Assistant" period, a way to provide
him some time to catch up on his work, ask for help on what he didn't
understand, and have a safe place to make sense of the fast-paced new
world of the U.S. middle school.

The door to my office flew open and I looked up, startled. Mr. Donalds stood there with a packet in his hand, his face red.

"What is this?" He yelled. "Don't ever modify my assignments!"

In his hand was a typed sheet that I immediately recognized.

The week prior, Jose had come into my office with eyes wide with fear and, in his hands, a thick stapled packet. The packet, copied by his Science teacher from some source or other, contained a 15-page in-depth description of the assignment for an upcoming mandatory science projects, a major portion of the semester's grade. Jose had handed it me, confusion in his eyes.

We sat down together and went through the document, which explained the scientific method, hypothesis formation, format for reporting, and so on...and on...and on! Mr. Donalds was old school. I knew him to be a very traditional teacher and the unofficial leader of the "I taught it — it's not my fault if they didn't get it," cult of teachers.

Jose and I had gone through the packet, section by section, reading it and talking about what each section meant. When we were done, we discussed what he understood about the project. We brainstormed ideas and stretched his still-developing facility with the language. We planned a project together, taking into consideration the limited resources of his family. When we were done, he had made a decision about his project and the steps that he needed to complete. I typed the steps that we identified in straight-forward language and gave them to him, promising him that as he worked his way through the process, he could ask for help as he needed it.

This was the offending document that the red-faced teacher waved in my face. In all honesty, my internal dialogue began with "Are you insane?" but

I moderated my inner voice with some effort, to talk this raging teacher off of his ledge. In the end, we talked through the situation. He acknowledged that Jose didn't have the language skills to understand the packet he had provided but maintained that every student had the same packet, arguing that was equal treatment. While it may have been, it was clearly not equitable given that Jose's experience and background placed him quite far behind his peers who had received the same packet. We agreed to meet together with Jose and that I would then continue to assist him in his "Office Assistant" periods. I hoped, at least, that our conversation would expand the understanding and empathy of this teacher.

In the end, Jose would continue to struggle academically, though we established a good rapport and continued to work together. I would also meet with his family to help them understand how they could assist him. He went on to high school the next year and he would continue to call to ask me to help him understand an assignment, the first of the year a memorable and perplexing assignment to read a Shakespearean play and write a paper on it.

Jose didn't have the academic background that our higher achieving students had. His language barrier got in the way of just about everything that he was asked to do. As a school, made it far harder for him to overcome these barriers than we had to. He was on a team of four teachers, the aforementioned science teacher notwithstanding, I also saw in stark form the impact that a teacher can make as his social studies teacher understood him, found ways to engage him in intellectual activity and conversation, and scaffolded the written texts that were so baffling to him. He loved her and thrived in her class, though when the bell rang, each day he skulked into his next period Science class, pulled his hood up, and prayed that no one would notice him.

A PLACE AT THE TABLE

It is critical that we think about the lived experience of our students, our coworkers and employees, as well as members of our larger society who do not look like us and whose backgrounds are different from ours. When I first became a principal, I saw blatant inequity in stark contrast. The kids who were referred to the office were largely students of color and those living in poverty. The children whose families were of the dominant culture tended to find easier success in school, speaking and operating in ways that resonated with educators who largely looked like them. When things went wrong, their parents had the agency and clout to advocate for them in systems that they understood and could navigate well.

Students of color in came into the school with the same intellectual capacity and motivation to succeed, but they often operated as foreigners in a system of schooling largely built on norms of the majority culture. They came into the school setting with the longstanding familial knowledge that these systems had as often been used to oppress them as lift them up. They found themselves too often in traditional classrooms where quiet adherence to authority and dispassionate, emotionally neutral discourse were valued above all else. Fierce debate, shared work and choral response, active exchange, and cultural language patterns were framed as traits to be molded out of them.

American schools have made efforts to do better, and while there are still far too few who have gotten it right, there are shining examples of success. For example, schools have embraced shifts in pedagogy and structure that expand access to rigorous courses to all students. Many have actively recruited a diverse teaching force so that not only do students see themselves reflected in the adults with whom they interact, but there are also different experiences in conversations at staff meetings, curriculum planning sessions, and even at the staff lunch table.

I led a school, for example, with a dynamic equity team that was comprised of a diverse group of smart and motivated educators. The team advised on school policies and conducted staff training. They were the heart and brain trust of the school. Their work was not easy but having a nucleus of staff who were laser-focused on equity meant that the faculty kept moving and getting better. And that was key. The explicit focus and acceptance that there was a problem was the first step in shifting practice in ways that changed things for kids.

During my prior years as a counselor, some of the students I worked with shared stories of grief over the loss of a grandparent, concern over their grades, or bullying, while others navigated more dire circumstances — physical and sexual abuse, the death of a parent, placement in foster care, or a life-threatening illness. And always in the midst of all this, there was a frustratingly steady stream of students who were experiencing crises that had their genesis in the school, issues that we had created. Most of these had something to do with equity and the very real struggles that students experienced in systems that were more about sorting and selecting than engaging and inspiring.

In my career, I have coached hundreds of leaders on equity-based practice. I have come to realize that doing this work requires either a strong sense of moral purpose or, in the absence of that, a system that ensures that equitable practices occur. While the former is certainly preferable, our students cannot wait for the adults in the system to "get it," so when the conditions don't exist for that, I'll take the latter.

To be fair, I don't believe I have ever met anyone who wakes up in the morning eager to harm the young people with whom they worked. In fact, most of the educators that I have encountered, even those whose actions had negative outcomes, thought they were doing right by their students.

These young people are our future. Their promise is our collective hope. The faces of real children and youth that we have failed come easily to mind for me — Monique, Alex, Marcus, Jose, and thousands more just like them, each from families who only wanted for them a rich, quality education that could spell transformation in their lives. They saw education, rightly so, as a bridge to a brighter future. For some, it was a path out of a bleak reality of limited opportunity, economic despair, and a host of negative social consequences. For their part, these young people were only limited by the systems in which they found themselves and the failure of their schools to lift them up and out.

I learned a lot from my work with students. Most of that was about courage, resilience, and forgiveness. Some of it, however, was about how our social system are, in fact, two (or more) systems. Some pave the way for those born, as the saying goes, on third base with the bases loaded. But others came to bat with a metaphorical leg tied behind them and were starting behind home plate.

Through years of advocating for students and shaping systems to support them, I began to understand equity at a deeper, more cellular level. It became the focus of my work, even if at first, I really didn't have a word for it. I just knew that something was awry, and that these remarkable young people, each full of promise and potential, had vastly different experiences of school. And I knew that was not just. I knew that we could do better.

Anyone who takes on a leadership role — be it at a school, community organization, governmental agency, corporation or, for that matter, a coffee shop, is going to have to grapple with this thing called equity. Really "getting it" changes how you interact with your staff, your clients or the public, and the kind of work that you choose to do that makes an impact.

I wish I could tell you it is easy work — that once I tell you the secret of equity, you'll have it down. But it's not that way. The truth is, equity work is hard work. If you find yourself grappling with it and struggling to get it right, making missteps along the way but staying in the conversation — then you are doing it right.

Equity-focused leaders are constantly checking themselves so that people influences by the systems that they lead don't experience different expectations or experiences based on arbitrary things like the color of their skin, their immigration status, or their zip code. It's damned easy, particularly for white folks like me, to slip back into the lull and embrace of privilege and to forget that privilege is denied to those who most need the leg up that it offers.

I should tell you right up front (though I'm betting that you already know this) that not everyone cares about this work. In fact, some think that this is the wrong work to do. They think that this work gives unfair advantages to those different from them; that it gives entitlements to lazy or just plain bad people, and that everybody should have the exact same treatment. These people are out there, and they do a whole hell of a lot of damage.

The best advice that I can give you, advice that has served me well, is to keep your sites clearly set on equity. Part of doing equity work requires maintaining that focus when you encounter that resistance. Because you will. Ensure that your work moves your system forward — influencing, in whatever way that you can, history's arc towards a more just and equitable world. It is worth whatever the cost.

MOONWARD BOUND

Every leader needs a kind of a compass, something that directs them to their own True North. There's a saying back in North Carolina where I grew up, "Know where your goat is tied." Okay, so I know that you probably don't have a goat — and if you do, big props to you from goat-lovers everywhere. Really.

But "knowing where your goat is tied" is about knowing who you are and what you stand for. It also means knowing what you would walk away for when the going gets tough. The wisdom in that old chestnut has proven itself to me time and again. So, my advice to you — whether you are already in a leadership role or are about to enter the rapids of leadership — is to know what you are about, know your "Why," and always know where the hell your goat is tied.

It is only too often that our very best intentions are shaded by unconscious bias and truth that reside outside of the periphery of our vision. Implicit bias is code for our deeply held assumptions about people. Who is good, who is bad? Who should be given the benefit of the doubt, who should be approached with a heavy dose of caution? What students just need a little more time, an extra push, or a call to home to get over hurdles when they struggle. Are there other students who, when experience the same struggle, earn instead an office disciplinary referral, a zero in the grade book, a lecture or, even worse, a well-meaning but misguided reduction in expectations?

There is a compelling body of research on *implicit bias* that gauges our initial responses to stimuli — positive or negative. Implicit bias is deeply baked into the cultural stew that makes us who we are and triggers before conscious thought kicks in. With awareness and practice, we can ameliorate its influence, but that starts with acknowledging and noticing its existence within us.

While there certainly are plenty of *explicit* forms of bias in our world, these *implicit* ones are often more pernicious. They are constantly operating and doing their dirty work beneath our consciousness. They emerge unbidden from our histories, our shared social constructs, and the meaning that we ascribe to our people and events.

We come, as we each must, to our lives and work seeing the world through the only lenses that we have, lenses shaped by our own histories, cultures, and experiences. Part of the leader's obligation is to ensure that public policy acknowledges our baked-in bias toward "otherness" and the pervasive and pernicious role that implicit bias plays. While our knee jerk, instinctive and implicit reactions to people do enough of their dirty work in our personal interactions, when they inform policy, their damage is far broader and more pernicious.

It is worth noting that this work requires humility and bringing our own full selves to the conversation. I have learned that as a white man who is by definition a beneficiary of privilege assigned to me based on the color of my skin and the cultural meaning attached to that in America, this work is about being an ally.

I was once the principal of a school where I had the good fortune of working with an articulate and courageous African American teacher who would come to be a close ally and thought partner in this work. I was honored to have very honest conversations with her around race. She would tell me that some days she was just tired — tired of being the one that had to speak up and call out implicit bias and racism when it occurred around the table in meetings and in social gatherings. She was tired of having to be, as she put it, "the angry black woman." She helped me understand the role that white allies play in shifting small, daily conversations that they have, the accumulation of which helps to shape, even in small pockets, our national discourse.

A teacher who always epitomizes excellence for me is one who inspired me as a middle-school student. Ms. Ryan was a young African American teacher — and she was kind of brilliant. She taught my junior high social studies class. She was intelligent, engaging, and she pushed me to understand that I was capable of doing more.

When Ms. Ryan approached me about entering an oratorical contest, I didn't hesitate to say yes to her, though in all honesty, I didn't really know at that time what an "oratorical" really was. Some sort of race, maybe? All I knew is that it sounded really important and so I agreed, hoping I would find out what it was before it was time to do it!

Over the following weeks, I would learn only too well what this contest was all about. I would write, revise, and rehearse a speech on the year's statewide assigned topic. Every step of the way, she was there behind me. She gave honest feedback, pushing me to make it better and then leaving me to revise, edit, and rehearse the speech before I brought it back to her.

When the day of the competition arrived, Ms. Ryan was there with me. When I won, I could see the pride in her face. She represents for me the best of what it means to be a teacher. In some ways, I have spent my subsequent career helping many hundreds of teachers to be just a little more like Ms. Ryan.

When I went to the finals of the competition later in the year, competing against wealthier, better dressed students from nearby private schools, I would come in second. I will never forget Ms. Ryan marching up to the judges and calling them out on violations of the rules that the winning student had committed, rules we had been painstaking to adhere to. While it didn't change the outcome, I will always remember how she stood up for me in that moment, something as valuable to me as the regional trophy that would have been mine. I suppose that the power of somebody standing up for you when they don't have anything to gain from it was somehow baked into my core that day. It is a lesson I never forgot.

She was a thinker who knew how to challenge each of us fortunate enough to learn at her feet. She brooked no foolishness but inspired in us a spark that she would deftly let take flame as she stepped back and let us find our way. She was the best example of what I teacher can be, and I remain in her debt to this day.

On September 12, 1962, John F. Kennedy challenged us collectively as a country to aspire to more:

> "We choose to go to the Moon in this decade and do the other things, not because they are easy, but because they are hard; because that goal will serve to organize and measure the best of our energies and skills, because that challenge is one that we are willing to accept, one we are unwilling to postpone, and one we intend to win."

Equity is our moonshot. Our schools are one of the last places where we come together, across lines of privilege, race, and class, to join together in common purpose. They are a crucible for the American dream of opportunity and promise. To be fair, schools suffer from differences in resources and, too often, expectations, but those that get it right are places of transformation. Attending a school like this shouldn't be a matter of the luck of the draw, but the right of every child.

We made our first moonshot. If we bring that same focus, imagination, and commitment, we can achieve this one, too.

chapter twelve

THE EQUITY PYRAMID

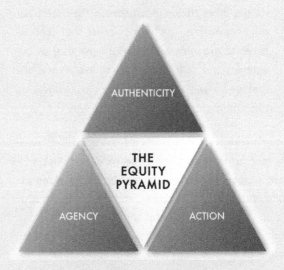

Figure 3.2 The Equity Pyramid

They were a tight crew. The school equity team met regularly to advise the school's leadership and faculty. The team read articles and books on critical race theory, examined exemplary practices, and discussed the lived experience of students and staff of color at their school. The work that they did was hard work. And it was important. Their school was not immune to the challenges of institutional racism.

They had each other's backs as the members advocated for equity in the school. Their meetings spaces were honest and safe. The members of this team had each other's backs and pushed one another in their work. They were allies that learned together, laughed together, and cried together. More, they had each other's backs — supporting one member as she reported that she had summoned the courage to speak out in response to a veiled racist comment in the break room when everyone else really just wanted to get through a pleasant lunch hour. This was what they did. They learned, and taught, and modeled what it meant to be an equitable leader. It was never-ending work and while they were never quite sure that they made a difference, they changed things.

Great leaders build teams that shift systems. They build a deep sense of cultural awareness and respect for all people. They build alliances, knowing when to roll up their sleeves and work alongside their teams and when to step out of the way. They show more than they tell. They guide more than they direct.

Great organizations have artful, equity-focused leaders that are courageous. When they have to, they are willing to take the unpopular stance. They show courage in ways both large and small.

True courage. We've too often mistaken bravado and posturing as courage. I have mentored many young leaders who had to learn the hard but critical lesson that leadership is not about ordering other people to do things, but to guide, listen, learn, and inspire. While these lessons come easier to some than others, they are the soft skills that are essential for leaders as they weather the storms.

It is invigorating to lead a team or an organization when things are going well — when an initiative is in the works, new staff are being on-boarded, or there is an uplifting speech or presentation to give. Then there are are other times, harder times, when there is hardly a whiff of an easy choice and when the stakes are at their highest and you as a leader are called on to make a tough call or have a confrontation you would just as soon not. These are times when doing the right thing and the easy thing are wholly different paths.

Here is the thing. Sometimes you *will* get it wrong. Sometimes you dishearten rather than inspire. Sometimes your motives are misinterpreted. Sometimes you give it your level best and fall short.

So err on the side of justice and moral purpose so that your bruises are worthwhile. Don't be shy of trying and keep at it. When it goes off the rails dust yourself off, re-grounding, and get back to the work on behalf of those you serve. Your leadership matters.

This Equity Pyramid for leadership can help you keep your leadership compass pointing to True North as you strive to be an artful, equitable leader.

AUTHENTICITY: BRINGING YOURSELF TO THE WORK

Equitable practice begins with who you are. Despite decades of misguided thought about equity work being about color-blindness, it turns out that was all along merely a mechanism to deny the pervasive impact that privilege and racism exert. While it may be easy to fail deny the impact of color when you live, as do I, in privilege, those who are marginalized by our shared social meaning ascribed to the color of their skin, their accent, or ethnicity, are only too keenly aware that color-blindness is really just racial tone-deafness and is a artifact of privilege, not a tool of equity.

Color-blindness assumes that race, color, and ethnicity don't matter and that everyone has an equal chance to achieve at the same level. When you exist in systems that have historically oppressed, though, that premise falls flat. The contexts of our lives, the social and racial realities of life, the pervasive impact of our shared sense of belonging and otherness, in fact, mean that we experience very realities throughout the daily conduct of our lives. Countering these differences begins with realizing that they exist.

Deep equity work begins with acknowledging one's own history and the unique lens of culture and experience through which we each view the world. When we acknowledge the existence and limitations of that lens and ensure that we are open and learning from others — engaging with those who have different cultures, experiences, and perspectives — we move, however incrementally, toward a more just society. The artful leader must approach equity work with a lens of humility that is informed by, and grounded in, others' experiences. Doing this work begins with acknowledging who you are and the social constructs that govern the ways in which you experience the world.

ACTION: DO THE DAMN THING

When I first came to equity work I did so out of a passion for social justice and a desire to make systems better for all. I believed, in those early days, that equity work was about getting others to embrace the moral imperative inherent in this work.

I came to understand, as I deepened my equity work as a principal, that the drive to help others find meaning in this work, while a worthy effort, was ultimately akin to pushing water uphill. People's own histories and belief systems, the continual churn of new staff, and the pervasive impact of privilege continually interrupted the process. I would come to understand the importance of just, well, doing the damn thing — doing something, evaluating it, and improving upon it next time. As rewarding as it is to change hearts and minds and while that work has to continue, systems can't wait to shift behavior, practice, and policy. We have to do the damn thing.

I came to understand that what we "do" is as much, or perhaps more important, than what we believe. In fact, while we continue the "why" work of changing belief systems, it is a pale counterpart to ensuring that equitable policies are implemented.

AGENCY: COURAGEOUS LEADERSHIP

I once had the good fortune to participate in a San Francisco Bay Area group of equity leaders from schools and school districts. This group was part learning community, part group therapy, and part activist society. Leaders — mainly leaders of color with a smattering of white allies such as myself — came together in a safe space to build community, share successes and failures, and learn and recharge before returning to the front lines.

Among a number of notable and memorable individuals in this group, there was an African American woman who spoke passionately about her work around equity in a neighboring school district. She said that she always kept in front of mind what she would walk away for. She argued, in fact, that everyone needed to know that about themselves. It empowered her to do courageous equity work in systems that were, frankly, never designed with that in mind. Her words were powerful and her conviction palpable. She inspired and pushed those of us gathered there to put our money where our proverbial mouths were and exemplified the courage that undergirds the equity component of the Artful Leadership Framework.

Deep equity work operates at once on both personal and professional levels. It is work that asks us not only to plan initiatives and shift practice, but also to explore our deeply personal conscious and unconscious biases and beliefs. In many instances, it requires us to confront those in some uncomfortable ways. Consequently, it is work that absolutely demands that we approach the work of leadership with humility, grace — and a heaping scoopful of courage.

This last one — courage — is a tricky thing in leadership. It can be easy to define as that X factor that propels leaders to take hard, unpopular stands that are right, though difficult. It is necessary when meeting the moment calls for speaking truth to power or challenging the status quo.

There are noble examples of courage that inspire, but courage also happens in small, ordinary ways on a daily basis. It happens in the break room when the choice is whether to be silent or to confront someone's unconscious bias. It happens when there is an opportunity to advocate for those who are denied a seat at the table and when it would be so much easier just to check your phone or shuffle papers.

It turns out that the "how" of our work is most often a mixture of humility, and a deep sense of conviction and courage that are as important as the "what" that we do.

chapter thirteen

IMAGINE...

How does an organization weave magic, creativity, and innovation into their daily at the cellular level? Disney is a shining example of an organization that gets this right. While the ethic permeates every level of the organization, the Imagineers are a study in leadership. In Disney parlance, engineers are Imagineers. They weave their vision and skill together in everything they do, designing experiences that amaze and inspire. They are something of a legend, these Imagineers. They are all masters of their respective crafts and they each bring something extra to the equation. Extra imagination. Extra creativity. That hard to define something...extra. They have been led by greats such as the renown Marty Sklar, a true Disney legend who recently passed away.

I had the great good fortune to meet Marty on a number of occasions and share a meal or conversation. He was one of the originals from Disneyland, there from the beginning and a remarkable individual who came to lead Disney Imagineering at the culmination of quite a storied career. Marty was inspiring and laser-focused on his "why." His leadership is a grand example of leadership as art. He spoke of the core principles that drove the Imagineers to be industry leaders and established the standards for their work. He never lost sight of the larger vision or purpose of making people happy, of making magic — no matter what the more mundane nature of the immediate "what" of the work at hand. His focus on solving problems, coupled with hard work, skill, ingenuity, and a heaping dose of creativity was a winning recipe — even outside the storied gates of Disney.

You've got to have focus as a leader and keep your eye on the proverbial ball. It is the only way to fire up those around you to move closer to their goals.

For well over a decade, I have served in upper-level leadership roles at County Offices of Education in California. The office where I led as Deputy Superintendent for twelve years served 23 independent school districts. The county was bimodal, with striking examples of both extreme afflu- ence and abject poverty. The excessive cost of living made the area all the more unpalatable for those in poverty's vice-like grip.

This dug at me. The test data largely looked okay. Scores were histori- cally better than state averages but when you dug in deeper and looked under the hood, all was not well. Something was amiss.

Historically underserved students — students of color, students living in poverty, English learners, and others were failed in great numbers by the very systems entrusted with serving them. Early in my tenure there, I grappled with this. Determined that we had to do something about it, I called my staff together early one Monday morning to discuss the plight that many of our children were in and what we were going to do about it.

Gathered with me were key division leaders, content specialists, and other leaders to imagine together what we might do to begin to stem the tide of this "achievement and opportunity gap," that seemingly intracta- ble gap in performance between identifiable groups of students. I challenged them that we had all we needed to make a difference — smart people, a solid infrastructure, and enough resources to support our work. There was one thing that I knew beyond a shadow of a doubt: We could no longer in good conscience sit by and do nothing.

The data at the county, state and national level painted a stark picture that African American and Latino students by and large came out on the losing end, while white and Asian students by and large performed at the higher end of the spectrum. We knew that this had nothing to do with the innate intellectual capacity or ability of either group but had something to do with how we imagined school and the kinds of opportunities that we had historically made available to them.

What I had seen for years as different treatment and experience at the student level as a counselor, and at the school level as a principal, suddenly came into stark context in terms of the scope of the problem when I began to look at the data more broadly.

"Not on my watch," I told them. "We are going to do something!"

It was a conversation that would drive our work for years to come. "But what will WE do?" I posed to these assembled thinkers and leaders, "What can we do together... us, here, in this moment, to change outcomes for youth?"

I knew we all held a firm ethic that it was possible and had conviction around this work. I had quite intentionally hired equity-minded individuals who were passionate about the work and about making a difference in the lives of underserved children in our community.

This small team began to imagine a variety of initiatives that would begin to shine a light on the plight of students in our county. We also wanted to establish a framework for a community of practice that would build a common language and vision for changing the conditions of learning for students throughout the county. There was palpable energy that day in the room — the kind of energy that materializes when passionate people are energized around solving intractable problems.

One of the signature pieces of this initiative, one that would take a central spotlight in this work was an event that came to be known as "Zap the Gap." It was a conference and community conversation on closing achievement and opportunity gaps. While a visible centerpiece of our strategy, we also were clear that a single event, even an impactful one, would not be enough to change systems. This was not the only, or, in some ways, even the most resonant component of this work. We were all about ensuring that equity-focused strategies were woven throughout the fabric of the instruction across our county.

It was exciting, passionate work that would expand over the next ten years from serving educators to bringing together communities and community leaders in a common space to build purpose and shared language. It was work that the local County Board of Education would come to engage deeply in, working to ensure that the dual front lines of this battle were fought in the classroom as well as at the policy level. We knew that one without the other was doomed to failure.

Ironically, years later, I would experience firsthand the pernicious, almost blinding power of white privilege. Ten years into this work that had shifted hearts, minds, and practice across the county, I would be called to defend this work during a political campaign that I had launched, a key cornerstone of which was my work around equity.

"Why do you continue this work when the achievement gap hasn't closed?" I was asked.

The small-minded racism that we had so fought against was in full flower in the perception that this was a side issue that should have a fix should be quick. "Check the box so and get back to our "real" work."

What those who held this view failed to understand was that the heart of this work was about creating a sense of community and shared language around our most vulnerable children. It was a focus that was necessary if we were to empower those working every day with children and youth to find solutions that worked in their context with their students. This work wasn't a about an event; but about a process we had to commit to over the long haul.

Over ten years, this initiative evolved from a small gathering of educators to an event that annually drew together hundreds of community leaders. Together we looked at data, heard from students, and had our thinking deepened by thoughtful, successful, and, sometimes provocative, guides.

We learned together about implicit bias. We spotlighted schools that were doing game-changing work with students who were failing elsewhere. We heard the eloquent and passionate real-life stories of students with whom others were not succeeding. We worked together as staff, board members, community leaders, and students to create something new, something that would make a difference in the lives of students who were desperate for someone to stand up for them.

It was deep work that helped till the soil in which a host of initiatives would grow to serve hundreds of thousands of students over time. While the needs persisted, the work helped shape a community of informed and engaged leaders who shared a common purpose and language and felt the moral imperative of this work. It was difficult, inspiring, and damned hard work that was not without its critics, those who often were steeped in a kind of privilege and bias that blinded them to the deep nature of what we were doing.

I have been guilty, at times, of taking for granted the bubble that I have lived in of those around me who "got" equity. There is a danger in assuming that there are shared understandings and commitments around this work in the world at large. The people that I spoke to on a regular basis had developed a shared vocabulary and understanding of the achievement and opportunity gaps. It went without saying that closing those gaps was the work that mattered most in our collective consciousness.

But I could take the heat and live to fight another day. The focal point of this work, the children — largely black and brown children — did not have that same luxury. They were living and often languishing in systems that were never designed to serve them and had historically failed to do so. They lost opportunities that would impact the course of their lives. I was the beneficiary of a privilege that allowed me to raise these conversations, even when it was difficult to do so. But these young people weren't just talking about it; they were living it.

It was for them that I did this work — and continue to do it. They are my vision and focus.

I would come to learn that even in the liberal California bubble in which I lived, there would always be those who thought that equity meant doing some special outing or activity designed for a small set of youth who had experienced particularly dire circumstances in their lives. The things that happened for these few children tended to be amazing and positive. However, they also made people blind to the failure writ large of the system to adapt and shift in ways that made the pathway to the American dream viable — and possible — for every child so that zip code, race, ethnicity, and socio-economic status were not predictors of success.

A STORY TO TELL

One of the partners and standard-bearers for this work that I would come to know was a remarkable gentleman named Bernard Kinsey. When I first encountered Bernard, I was floored by the power of his work. He is a fascinating human being, an eloquent, insightful, and accomplished visionary. A retired executive from Xerox, he and his wife Shirley have spent their lives assembling a stunning collection of African American artwork and primary source documents that tell of seminal African American contributions to the American story.

It is difficult to capture in words the power of Bernard and the stories he tells. These stories are quite literally whitewashed out of our textbooks in favor of more traditional, and largely white, stories. Bernard's telling of these forgotten stories is poignant, whether in person or in his text *The Kinsey Collection*.

Bernard talks about what he calls the "Myth of Absence." The absence of these stories from our recorded and taught curricula is telling in itself. What is most troubling about that concept are the messages that absence communicates to young people of color about their value and worth.

Bernard's message speaks to our obligation to break down racial barriers and increase access to the levers of power to communities of color. In a March 2013 article in *Forbes*, Bernard's comments from an executive leadership series are recounted, "Leave the door open and the ladder down," he said of the imperative to pay it forward and create opportunities for those who will follow.

Leaders like Bernard, who are equal part story tellers and guides, change the conversation across our country. The story he tells is a powerful, inspiring — and troubling — one in its stark absence from our recorded history. Along my journey to artful leadership, I find inspiration in leaders like Bernard that are sterling models of artful leadership.

Like Bernard, embrace your work with a sense of humility and honor the contributions of those who came before. Commit to increasing access and opportunity to systems or structures of power to those who do not look like you and whose voices have been silenced. We will all be better for it.

Leaders who have a clear sense of purpose stay focused even when the mundane demands of leadership materialize. I have a long-standing practice of taking time at the beginning of staff meetings to spend a few minutes taking turns sharing equity perspectives.

Now, I have rarely come across a staff meeting agenda that wasn't over-full full of issues to resolve, input to solicit, and details to iron out. There is just never enough time to get to it all. But I've learned not to start there. Devoting a few minutes to share experience around equity refocuses the team on the vision that animates us in our work. Whichever leader's turn it is takes a few minutes sharing something personal about herself. Some share cultural norms or personal experiences from their background. Some people bring a resource or issue to discuss. This simple commit-ment of a few minutes out of our day helps teams to know each other better and understand the strength that lies in the multiple perspectives that we bring to the work.

These moments of sharing have been poignant or painful on occasion. People share personal histories of racism and bias. One gentleman shared his family's experiences with Japanese internment and the per-vasive imprint that it left on them all. Others share joyful experiences of their cultural roots and traditions. They all helped us to deepen our team and to better know one another not only as professionals, but as human beings on a shared journey.

Focus on your purpose, whether it is to make people happy or to make them free. Do what it takes to remind yourself why you and the people you lead are doing what you do. Just like those Disney Imagineers that bring creativity and imagination to the practice of their craft, so must we as leaders. Just imagine what is possible!

Be artful. Be philosophical. Find a deep, humanity-enhancing reason for what you do every day, no matter how mundane the details of your work are and inspire those around you to share that purpose too. It is worthy work.

chapter fourteen

UPSTREAM

L iz and Jose are picnicking on the bank of a rushing river, basking in the symphony of the waters. Just between the egg salad and brownies, they looked up in alarm as they hear a scream and see a person flailing in the water and being swept down the river towards them.

Without hesitating, Liz and Jose leap into action. Liz grabs a downed tree branch from the bank as Jose wades out into the river. Liz holds one end of the branch to prevent him from being swept away in the angry current. With effort, the person caught in the rapids grabs the end of the branch and Jose and Liz together pull him from the water. The three collapse in a pile of exhaustion, gratitude, and relief.

Almost immediately, though, they look up in alarm as another scream comes from the river. Leaping into service, the small ragtag crew rallies together and heroically saves the young girl flailing in the river's rapids. Soaking and exhausted, the four gasp for breath on the river bank. With shock, they start as another scream comes from the river. They are at a loss — there are just too many people drowning in the river to possibly save them all.

Liz watches as Jose and the two people they pulled from the water summon the strength through their exhaustion to try yet another time. Liz doesn't help them this time. She turns and walks up the riverbank.

"Where are you going?" Jose shouts in a panic.

"I'm going upstream," Liz yells back to him, "to see why they are falling in the river in the first place!"

Liz walks up the bank of the river, where she finds a collapsed bridge from which people are falling into the water. Enlisting her friends, they post warning signs and begin to repair the bridge, knowing that there were just too many people falling into the river for them to save them all downstream. But upstream, they can make a difference.

Some version of this metaphor about the differences between upstream and downstream work has appeared in a variety of forms in literature and trainings from the health sector, such as in the writings of John D. Stoeckle around healthcare in the late 1960s. It resonates with the work of just about any system — schools, corporations, philanthropic organizations, government. By nature, we tend to be problem solvers and focus our energies where there is a crisis, putting out fires and managing problem. But when we shift the focus to proactive, preventive action, we might just find the sweet spot for realizing change.

In America's schools, this notion of upstream work helps us understand our shared focus on closing what we used to call the "Achievement Gap," that disturbingly predictable gap in achievement between groups of students. It turns out that these gaps in achievement were really a result of gaps in opportunity and resources that are applied to schools. All of these contribute to an opportunity cost that these students bear. But they don't have to. All of these things are results of choices we have made about what we value, about what matters to us.

Transforming systems, it turns out, is tricky work. Let me give you an example.

My first principalship was at a suburban school in North Carolina. It was a good school. There were skilled teachers, an engaged parent community, and it was reasonably well-resourced. There were some really awesome kids who came, quite literally, from both "sides of the tracks" in a town where railroad tracks, quite literally, divided affluent and impoverished communities. It was a good school — and it had the potential to be a great school. I was struck with how smoothly things operated and how effective the school was for most of its kids. Nevertheless, I began to see the potential to improve learning, especially for students of color, students living in poverty, and English learners.

We set out charting a course forward to take this "good," very traditional school to greatness. Inherent in that conversation was some risk that we would lose the momentum of the school's long-established traditions. I was a new principal at the school. Could we do it?

The idea was to create a learning community by trusting the staff to move out of their comfort areas and learn new ways of approaching both their content and their students. After all, while there were a good number of newer teachers on board, there was also a strong core of veteran teachers who were, frankly, exceptional at what they did. Would they engage in this process to think differently about the work? What would that process be like for them?

We spent our first year together calibrating, selecting an approach that we all believed in and that had the potential to move the needle for students. Teachers were clustered in teams that would engage in deep book study of the concepts with an expert guide. Together, we rolled up our sleeves to get to work.

Over the course of the next year, teachers began implementing the new instructional methodology that we were studying. Our broader, full roll-out was still some months away. We were also putting into place a system of peer coaching that we would use to support the learning and expected ups and downs of trial and error as we shifted practice. Slowly, pockets of teachers became excited by what we were learning together and began to implement the model in a classroom here and there. A community around this new way of learning began to emerge. It was an exciting time, seeding a new way of thinking about our work.

By the time the following year came, there were only a few hold outs. Some of these were veteran teachers who achieved consistently good results with students and were, in many ways, the backbone of the school. I knew that real change wouldn't happen without them on board. All of our work and commensurate gains would be lost. I recall clearly when one of them boldly proclaimed that this new workshop approach couldn't happen in her grade level. The needs were too great and the differences in students' abilities too broad ranging. The curriculum too demanding, she said. I made her an offer that in retrospect was pretty naive.

"Give me your literacy block for a week," I told her. "Maybe you're right. Let me come and teach your class in this way for a week and see if you're right or if it can work." She looked at me skeptically, one eyebrow arching up.

With a smirk that only a veteran teacher can give when presented with such an outlandish offer, she said, "You're on."

While I had spent years working with groups and classes of students in counseling and guidance lessons, I had never been a literacy teacher. I was faced with not only the complexity of implementation, but the added wrinkle of managing the transition from what was a very well-established, traditional approach to learning to this new, decentralized model. I began to ponder the seemingly elusive wisdom of — sometimes — just keeping my mouth shut. That's never really been my thing, though.

Could I even do it? If it failed, it could unbalance the entire initiative. This particular teacher was experienced...and vocal; an opinion-leader in the school. I had the distinct impression that the rumor mill was in full gear when I volunteered to take on her class. But... no pressure!

I set about a frantic week of planning. I selected texts, created decentralized classroom structure and rotating literacy schedules, generated organizing graphic displays, planned mini writing lessons, and studied the students' assessments. All of these were systems and processes that we had been learning together. I believed in them, but they sounded a lot simpler in the safe confines of professional development sessions.

In the end, it was an exhausting but successful week. Each day, I hurried through my morning demands of the principalship in time to be in the classroom for a two-hour literacy block. Then I returned to my afternoon of lunch supervision, meetings, disciplinary referrals, parent calls, district reports, and the thousand other demands on an elementary principal's time before preparing for the next day and providing feedback on student work.

The students, by and large, got what we were doing and enjoyed the freedom to read books that interested and challenged them and to write and revise their work more independently. The teacher eyed me from her desk at the corner of the room the entire week, looking up now and then from her grading and planning. She didn't say a word to assist or intervene, though.

When the week was nearing a close, she said, "You know, I still can't say I really know how to do all of this, but I see it can work. And if you were willing to go to this much effort, I'm game to give it a try." She was to become one of my most vocal cheerleaders, quickly correcting less veteran teachers who made the mistake of commenting that this new type of instruction couldn't be done.

It was a win that had also given me a renewed appreciation for what I was asking my teachers to do. Changing practice and implementing new ways of teaching was hard work. As hard as it was for me, it was harder still for these experienced teachers who were good at teaching and had done it for many years. The final push into critical mass for this project came at the hands of two of the teachers who were the backbone of the school. They were skilled, but skeptical, and continued to offer their instruction in the way that they had for 25+ years.

At a staff meeting at the end of the first year of implementation, I presented the prior year's achievement results which just had come out to the staff. To the collective "oohs and aahs" of those who had worked their fingers to the bone to implement our new system, I shared with pride the trajectory of our student achievement. Every grade level had (remarkably) spiked sharply up. While the performance of all subgroups, including our highest achieving groups of students, had climbed, that of our lower-performing groups of students had shot up even more dramatically.

It was an authentic moment of celebration and relief for a staff that had worked hard to make this happen based on faith and a belief that it would make a difference. We were prepared for what is known as the "implementation dip" that happens when something new is implemented. But, to our relief and delight, our kids had amazed us.

However, there was one exception. The 5th grade teachers had a slight decline in their achievement, a stark contrast on the graph in comparison to the rest of the school. We didn't linger on that during the meeting or shame them but got on with our planning for the coming year.

As I walked out of that staff meeting and back towards my office, my sixth sense told me someone was behind me and I looked to see the two veteran 5th grade teachers following me, the ones who had stuck to their tried and true way of teaching.

Following me into my office, they closed the door and said "Look, we don't really know how to do this or what it should look like. We have taught for a long time and know what we are doing. We have had success with our students. But numbers don't lie. We want our students to have what the others are obviously getting. We want to learn."

That conversation began an exciting year of collaboration and growth. These two teachers, strong and skilled backbones of the school, transformed into instructional leaders. They never fully gave up their tried and true style, but they infused it with new energy, ideas, and practices. They became champions and cheerleaders for this new kind of instruction and, without saying much, clearly communicated to the remainder of the staff that this was just how things worked here now.

In two years' time, the gaps between historically higher and lower achieving student groups diminished from forty-two percent to eight percent while the achievement of all student groups rose. The results made the difficulty and challenge of doing this kind of work worthwhile and cemented in me the knowledge that achievement and opportunity gaps are not baked into the system. They are the result of choices that we make in classrooms and schools across America. Through hard work, commitment, and focus, we could change the trajectory in ways that improved all students lives.

Changing systems can happen. And it is exciting when it does!

STANDING TOGETHER

It was only a couple of years later that I would move across the country from NC to California to assume the helm of a school similar in size, but different in just about every other way.

While my past school had been cohesive, with strong systems and a robust teamwork spirit firmly in place, this one was fractured. You could feel the angst, stress, and trauma when you walked in the doors. An embattled principal had recently been removed after a concerted campaign by parents and staff, and the school still reeled from the experience.

While there were some innovative, remarkable teachers, there were also some who were weak and caused me to wonder how they had ever ended up choosing a profession working with children all day. You know the type – those who just really didn't seem to like them very much at all. Nevertheless, here I was, so I began meeting with them all, one on one. I met with the louder voices among them as well as those who had just kept their heads down and tried to do their work and, as I did, I began to understand their perspectives and began to build bridges.

One asset that existed in this school was a quite remarkable equity team made up of passionate and focused teachers (many of whom had been on the interview panel that hired me). I remember them well — Mefula, Roz, Evalina, and Jamie, among others. I was honored to join their tight knit team that was huddled to lead the site's deep, equity-based work. These courageous and unflinching equity champions were committed to all of the students of the school — as well as to their colleagues. They were focused on the *possible* and the *just*, their gaze firmly fixed beyond the strictures of the current reality. I learned a lot from them as we rolled up our sleeves together and did the hard work of shifting a school to more equitable practice.

Together we planned professional learning activities for staff, analyzed data, read and discussed challenging thought pieces on equity, and guided this somewhat fractured school through not only its healing, but its growth. We led activities that pushed the staff to explore our biases and assumptions about others.

We would come together when an equity-laden incident would occur at the site. We supported each other when the work became overwhelming, the payoffs too sporadic, and the pushback too intense. We functioned as something of an equity version of a basketball team. Various members stepped up to take the lead when others needed to fall back. We were honest with each other in a way that transcended roles, and we worked out of a space of deep trust.

This team had a dramatic impact on student achievement as well as the climate of the school. Over just a couple of years, the achievement lines on our site data graphs arced up for every single student subgroup. Every one. We were thrilled! The student body writ large achieved the state's benchmark target for success for the first time in the school's history. What we were doing was working.

I learned a lot from that team. I learned that that equity work is difficult when done well and that you'd better damned well have allies. Carrying the torch alone is daunting, exhausting, and wears even the most inspired torchbearers down. Many of the bonds forged as we walked through the fires together last still to this day. That's how durable meaningful partnerships are.

If you are privileged enough to be a leader in a school, you may have your own story of what has made a difference for your kids. Share them. We all get better when we learn from others' successes — and failures. America's students are our greatest resource. They are bright, full of promise, and with something important to say. They are wonderfully diverse, bringing their unique perspectives, cultures, and experiences to the last truly shared space in American life, the public school. They are the hope for our tomorrows and the promise of today.

We shortchange too many in classrooms across this country. Getting this right is truly our greatest hope to touch the future, not only for those students who want only the opportunity to excel, but for a society in which success is not an artifact of the color of your skin, the size of your bank account, or your native language. The work of equity, our "why," is a critical component of the framework for artful leadership. And whether your leadership work is in schools, corporations, non-profits, or small businesses — leading in ways that create more equitable and socially just conditions of life and learning for all of those that we are privileged to serve makes the work worth whatever effort is required.

chapter fifteen

EMPATHIC DESIGN

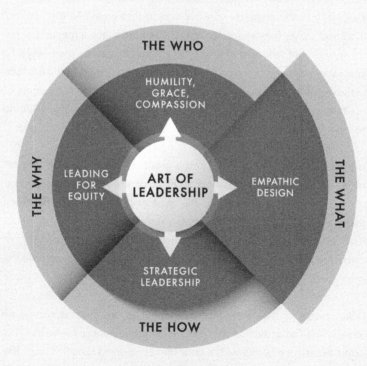

Figure 4.1, Empathic Design

I had the opportunity on a couple of occasions to meet Mark Sumner, a legendary Imagineer at Disney, and hear him speak about his design experience. The well-chronicled story of his design process for the Disneyland (and subsequently the Disney World) attraction that was initially called "Soarin' Over California" is the stuff of legend.

The concept for the ride, Sumner tells, emerged from the vision to create a ride that captured the flight experience, thrust guests into flight through stunning vistas, and let them leave their land-bound lives behind and soar to the heavens (at least for a few minutes).

Mark describes the team's design process and initial attraction designs, one of which involved multiple floors of theatre type seats that were to jut out into the immense concave screen that would fill their field of vision and create the experience of flight. He describes a meeting at the end of weeks of planning at which they determined that there were no acceptable solutions to the problems plaguing the design — the logistics involved with getting so many guests up and down to multiple floors of an attraction non-stop all day. Mark left that meeting on Friday with the growing realization that the entire concept was about to be scrapped.

Over the weekend, though, he had a brainstorm and climbed into his attic to retrieve his childhood erector set, complete with its metal braces, nuts, and bolts. Mark engaged his skill as an engineer, fueled by his vision for the experience of the end user. Breakthrough came: an arm would raise rows of seats up into the air, allowing not only immersion into the environment of the screen, but also gentle movements to accentuate the sensation of flying through the impressive skyscapes.

Mark created, in that weekend, the ingenious design that served as the model for an attraction that has delighted audiences for years. This design experience began with a clear and compelling vision of what the experience of the end-user would be, the experience of flight. The ingenuity and skill came in finding the right path to get there. That is what leadership is all about.

Good leaders know how to move systems and solve seemingly intractable problems. Those without that focus just maintain the status quo and keep the hamsters running on their little wheels. That isn't good for systems, and really isn't a good situation for the hamsters, either!

My thinking on the "what" of leadership evolved. Early on, I had a fondness for strategic planning in its penchant for strict organization and linear design. I still remember the huge binder that spelled out the process and provided the worksheets and systems to make it work. I remember, too, going through those processes with the various layers of meetings, planning documents, and the resultant cumbersome plans that too often ended up on an office bookshelf, never to see the light of day again.

It was like some sort of cosmic recipe from on high for changing systems. Except that too it didn't change much of anything.

Time after time, I heard well-meaning leaders speak about making these documents "living plans" that would drive practice. Then I watched them fall when faced with the gravitational pull, the inertia, of doing things the way we have always done them.

These days, I think of the "what" of good leadership more like a master artist — bringing some skilled hands, a high-quality canvas, the necessary pigments and brushes, and just the right dose of inspiration to the task. From these disparate parts, the master artist strives to create something lovely, important, and lasting. The artist may create something that takes your breath away, stirs you to action, or even stirs things up.

So does the leader. It is with that mindset of the master artist that I have come to approach the design, or the "what," of leadership.

The best process, the kind of design that we are talking about, begins with careful attention to the people for whom this newly created thing is intended, be it an initiative, product, or service. Doing this well requires deep understanding of people's needs, hopes, and dreams. Without that kind of thoughtful approach, the whole process and investment of energy, time, and resources are for naught.

I've seen far too many well-meaning leaders design initiatives with the best of intentions that come from their own grey matter — or from their tight circle of like-minded thinkers. Often, it is totally divorced from the messy treasure pile that is the lived experience of the user.

And it is messy. Ask a person who will be the recipient of a program or the user of a product what they really need and how it should work, and you will hear a lot of things you never expected. It's work that requires some humanity, empathy, and skill.

This work produces a kind of authenticity that emerges from genuine inquiry. It begins with empathy for the lived experience of stakeholders that permeates the design. In *Big Magic: Creative Living Beyond Fear*, Elizabeth Gilbert observes that "the older I get, the less impressed I become with originality. These days, I'm far more moved by authenticity. Attempts at originality can often feel forced and precious, but authenticity has quiet resonance that never fails to stir me." I think she got that right.

Not every design or leadership challenge will work out spectacularly. Yet when a leader begins with the perspective of the end user's experience firmly in mind and couples that with the skill and mastery of a discipline, truly spectacular things can happen — and you can, it turns out, soar.

chapter sixteen

MAVERICKS

Outside the solid wall of windows, the waters were blue and calm, belying their location. Just beyond the breakwater, the Mavericks lay, their historic waves the stuff of legend. Surfers from across the globe came to try to tame them.

Just north of the town of Half Moon Bay, California, at the unassuming village of Princeton-by-the-Sea, is the Mavericks. After a storm on the Pacific Ocean, the waves routinely crest over 25 feet and have been known to reach 60 feet or more. It is a storied place from which some surfers emerged in triumph, some in gratitude, and from which some did not return.

On this fall day, there was a nip in the air and few clouds in the crisp sky. Inside, the managers reconvened from their small group work, assembling in a meeting room with its striking wall of windows looking out onto the Pacific Ocean. One group bustled as they carried their chart paper in from the patio where they had gathered around a cold fire pit. An excited chatter punctuated their return to the room. Others taped chart papers to the windows, momentarily blocking the spectacular view with words, diagrams, and graphics.

Each work group consisted of leaders from the instructional division of the county office of education where I served as Deputy Superintendent. While our retreat was an annual event, this one was different. Managers worked in small groups to identify innovations that had emerged from empathy-based conversations around their lived experiences as leaders in the division. Their conversations were structured around interviewing a member and letting him or her share pain points and wonderings. Then they designed a prototype solution together. Their conversations were inspired, lively, and passionate.

One group designed a pilot project for managing remote work, a new concept for the somewhat bureaucratic organization in which they operated. Another crafted a system to structure and manage cross-departmental work groups across divisions that would align together around specific content. Their ideas were delightfully imperfect, their exploration creative and ripe for prototyping, testing, and adjustment. But the kernels of the thing were there, new and creative and out of the box. And that was the point.

There in the shadow of the historic Mavericks waves, they were tapping into the kinetic power of creativity, the kind that demands courage, suspension of judgement, and, above all, trust in the process — and people.

Leading this motley crew of smart, innovative managers involved helping them to manage the tension some felt between high stakes, heavy work volume, and a body of work that was largely governed by statute. Their "what" was fairly well established. The "how" was a horse of a different color and required them to be courageous and innovative, creatively strategic, and playful in their prototyping. It was a different kind of design process that varied from the more traditional and staid strategic planning protocols to which they were more accustomed. It was inspired by their own deep experiences in their work and was informed by empathy, humility, and a willingness to think as a designer rather than as a middle manager.

When I work with leaders who are new to this sort of approach to planning and design, it sometimes takes a minute to nudge them into their own realization that many of our traditional models of leadership and decision-making are artifacts of another time. This design conversation asks leadership to know themselves and to be, very genuinely, who they are. It requires a switch from acting to serve your own purposes — be they financial, philanthropic, or altruistic — to being grounded in service to others. That is the spoke around which the rest of the systems rotate.

The notion of leadership as a lofty position has always escaped me. Even the more singular public moments — such as speaking before thousands of people or launching a bold new initiative — aren't the real stuff of leadership. That is all about inspiring people to be their best or do something new in the service of others. It is a stance of service, at its heart.

Many of the new leaders that I have mentored come to the conversation with a primal fear of the moment when someone challenges them, refuses to comply with their brilliant edict, or actively opposes them. Their mental model of what leadership looks like doesn't square with these things. And, to be sure, these things do occur from time to time, even for veteran leaders. The problem isn't the existence of these things; it is knowing how to respond to them genuinely.

Artful leadership is a messy mix of grace and humility. Greatness, it turns out, isn't a destination at which you arrive by prescribed steps. It has little to do with the degrees you have, the commendations you have received, or the posts you have held. Greatness is about the depth of your humanity and the skill with which you help people to be their best and believe in things that they didn't think were possible. That is work that requires skill and a heaping dose of humility. It also requires a streak of the maverick.

Let me introduce you to a maverick I once knew: a great, empathic educator and a great friend.

chapter seventeen

PEAS AND CARROTS

C heryl was a hoot, with a special brand of crazy that drew everyone to her, never knowing what her next adventure might be.
She was a feisty, red-headed firecracker who would tell it like it
was, no holds barred, the unvarnished truth. She was also an unflinching
advocate for kids on the margins.

Cheryl was known to do some crazy things, on occasion. She once wrote
the IRS a letter, telling them that it was time to break up and thank-
ing them for their time together but notifying them that she would like
to cancel her subscription. On another occasion, she dressed up as her
80-year-old, fictional Aunt Hessie, mask, cane, and shawl, after convinc-
ing her beloved superintendent that she was bequeathing the school
district a million dollars for some oddball project. Only Cheryl could get
away with these things.

Everyone who knew Cheryl loved her zany spirit and her unapologetic
commitment to her students. She was also my confidant and trusted
friend. But to tell you only these things would be to miss a great part
of who she was. She had a great heart, particularly for the underdog,

whether they were children on the margins or a person who had been dismissed by others as irrelevant.

She was an alternative school principal who was a fierce advocate for her kids. Others may have given up on them, but Cheryl never did. Along the way, she saved countless lives of young people who were well on their way to increased involvement with the juvenile justice system, dropping out of school, and other negative outcomes of being lost in the system.

She knew a thing or two about empathy. In fact, she was kind of an empathy savant when it came to children and youth on the margins. She innately saw their worth and potential. She had in spades that elusive ability to understand how someone else was feeling. She would deploy that skill, to sometimes spectacular (or spectacularly annoying) effect, depending on your point of view. She was a school administrator committed to understanding and connecting with students as people regardless of whatever infraction might have landed them in her office. She was known for her connections with kids who struggled in school, many of them students of color in the alternative school in which she worked, whom most everyone else had quite long since given up on. She saved more students than she ever knew, subtly altering the trajectories of countless lives by the depth of her caring.

It has been my experience that empathy is more than an admirable character trait. It is a verb, a way of doing that is inspired by understanding. When you encounter someone who leads with empathy on a daily basis and for whom deep understanding of others drives their daily practice, it is hard not to be struck by the power and deep goodness that they exude. Don't get me wrong, empathy is a skill and habit of mind that leaders can grow, and it is the fuel to realizing your vision and achieving greatness.

It is worth noting that the skills of empathy, the focus on keeping the main thing the thing, and of not taking the rest too seriously are powerful skills for leadership, but they are also skills for life. Both of these can be tested — and, sooner or later for all of us, will. So, build the skills now, deepen the relationships that matter, and do good work grounded in this deep way of knowing. Like me, strive to be just a little more like Cheryl each day, and you will do unimaginably good work.

Cheryl carried her good humor and empathy into her final challenge of life as she faced breast cancer. On a late July afternoon, the day after her birthday, when I had flown across the country to surprise her, we talked, sitting on the porch of her sister's cabin in the woods.

We both knew it would be our last day together. Her cancer had progressed, and she was newly feeble and relegated to a wheelchair and connected to an oxygen tank. I would fly home to California the next day. We both felt the time passing far too fast. We laughed and joked a bit, uncomfortable small talk filling the space between us of things unsaid. The afternoon began to wane and the realization was heavy in the air that it was nearly time to say goodbye. I told her, falling back to the honesty that had defined our friendship, that I didn't want to let her go.

"Don't you want me to have peace?" she asked, grasping my hand.

There was a pause. "How about peas?" I asked, searching for some shred of the lightness that we had shared but that had abandoned us on this day.

"Well, if it is peas and carrots, then okay," she said, that old twinkle returning to her eye for just a moment. We both collapsed in laughter — one last time.

It was a moment of grace, of lightness, in an afternoon otherwise washed in tears of mortality, loss, and grief. Yet it was an oddly fitting way to say goodbye — two great friends understanding that their story, or at least this part of it, was at an end.

As Cheryl so vividly exemplified, empathy is not just a mindset or character trait. It is a real thing that can live and breathe in the daily work of leadership. It came to mind recently when I was coaching an aspiring leader who was struggling with understanding empathy. This bright young woman had a mind for data and saw numbers and systems in quite complex and brilliant ways. The ways of people, however, sometimes confounded her.

After we'd had a lengthy discussion of empathy and its role in design, she came to me, perplexed.

"I don't get it," she said. "So, if I have an employee who is late to work and I use empathy to understand that they are having childcare issues, well, don't they *still* have to come to work on time?"

This aspiring leader was hitting a hurdle that every new leader has to traverse. It has to do with the art of balancing empathy with problem-solving and accountability. Those things, I explained, aren't mutually exclusive. As we talked, I saw understanding dawn on her that knowing someone's lived experience doesn't mean that problem solving doesn't have to occur to ensure that the needs of the organization are also met. In fact, both of those things can occur simultaneously. We role-played the kinds of questions that she might ask this hypothetical employee and I saw a light trigger in her — understanding was a human "way of being" as a leader. It frames the kinds of conversations that leaders have and provides context for their decision-making.

A LISTENING STANCE

Empathy is a skill that the leader can use to design work that is impactful, relevant, and meaningful. It is a leadership stance that begins with some basic skills and beliefs. For example, the artful leader has to master the fine art of listening to understand. Sounds easy, right? Turns out, not so much.

When you are particularly passionate about your own ideas, especially the most brilliant ones, it is far too easy to slip into the trap of only listening to prepare your next argument. That isn't the kind of listening we're talking about. But what is critical is genuinely listening to understand. And that is a muscle that leaders have to build.

Back when I was a middle school counselor, I led mediations with students in conflict. We would start with one student sharing her story of whatever tragic middle school drama, real or imaged, had transpired. Then, the person they were in conflict with repeated it back to them until the first person could say, "Yes, that's how I feel. You understand."

Believe me, when two middle school students have been in argument or conflict of some other sort, retelling the other person's story without judgement, negative affect, eye-rolling, or other attitude took some work — and sometimes a few tries before they got it right. Then it was their turn to share their version of events. Only when both affirmed that the other understood where they were coming from could they move into the next phase and begin to establish agreements to resolve the conflict.

That kind of listening is the foundation on which empathic leadership is built. It is a skill and a habit — and it takes work. So, well...listen up.

chapter eighteen

THE FLYING SCHOOL BUS

O nce upon a time there was a flying school bus. Imagine it: a psy-chedelic school bus, loaded with kids that would land at various national parks and natural ecosystems to provide a mechanism for kids to learn about our environment.

When the team members told me about it, I reacted kind of like how I imagine you just did.

"Come again?" I said as I peeked in everyone's coffee mugs to see just what they were imbibing that morning.

Okay, so maybe the flying school bus wasn't real — but the idea of it was and, in the proper context, it was the kind of idea that sparked creative leadership and inspired a team to imagine something new.

Technically, it was a prototype that emerged from a design challenge around environmental education/literacy. The process had begun some months earlier with convening a host of district and community leaders to do some blue sky thinking around what was possible. And while this process produced some interesting ideas, there was still something missing — some overarching purpose and process. From there, a process emerged that resulted in, among other things, the aforementioned flying school bus.

My work at the time had focused me on a need to expand environmental education offerings throughout the county. While we had a well-established and highly respected outdoor education program that decades of children had attended, the attention to environmental education beyond that was spotty at best. It was largely an artifact of a random environmentally motivated teacher here or there. It was not in any way systemic.

Our team was inspired and imagined something more. I knew that we could do our normal thing, which was to dig into some research, get smart people together who knew the field, and put together a plan. It was the standard way that we solved problems and, in lots of instances, produced OK results. The problem was that however robust such a plan might be it would be missing some critical components — the input, thinking, and eventual buy-in of those who did the work and, most importantly, those whom it would impact.

For this initiative to take off, we had to think outside of the box and engage our most creative muses. We needed to develop a plan that was inspiring and that excited and engaged participants. How would we get there?

We needed to think differently about our work, and that required getting us out of the traditional mindsets and into more generative, creative spaces. We assembled a team of thinkers, each coming from different perspectives, to put this plan together.

The broader work began with loosening up the team's mental muscles and attitudes towards innovation. A skilled design/process consultant put the group through their design paces, blending design, music, art, and improv to create a space in which our creativity could thrive.

The team practiced empathy interviewing, active listening, and focused reflection. Then we gathered quite a motley crew of stakeholders — teachers, administrators, community members, organizational heads, and even students.

In small groups, we interviewed individuals who came from very different perspectives on the subject of environmental literacy. We sought to understand their experiences and perspectives about what they needed around environmental literacy. The groups then analyzed what they heard and began reflecting on what they had heard.

The flying school bus wasn't the only prototype to emerge from this process. There were also converted parks with living ecosystems, biodomes in schoolyards, and school-based "pizza gardens" that grew ingredients that would wind up on a pizza.

All of these oddball designs emerged from small mixed teams tasked with engaging deeply in empathy around the needs of one individual. They were to brainstorm freely and without limitations. The physical prototypes they made to share with the larger group were constructed of a hodgepodge of materials — chairs, pie tins, pipe cleaners, pompoms, cardboard, construction paper, markers, and string.

It was an assortment of stuff perfectly suited for any five-year-old's birthday party extravaganza. Except it wasn't for such an event, it was for the group of serious, studied, and accomplished adults. Unfiltered and unlimited by realities or boundaries, groups were to create a mockup prototype of their solution.

Over the next few weeks, our small design team analyzed each of these prototypes. Together, we pondered what each team had been getting at. The ideas were oddball and implausible, playful and outlandish, and they opened a doorway for us to more deeply understand what mattered in this work. What would emerge from this work was a robust model that was grounded in a series of "guideposts," or organizing principles, that had been mined from the prototypes. From this framework, an innovative environmental literacy approach emerged that would come to engage the community, involve partners, and expand learning for children and youth throughout the county.

And it was all thanks, in large part, to a flying school bus. The team that had designed the school bus was trying to get at a solution that was innovative, informative, and playful, engaging students actively and actually getting them into the various environments about which they were learning. In their oddball project was the kernel of the idea upon which the eventual model would rest.

This kind of design experience can be applied to just about any sort of project. Its principles informed a team that I led in building a statewide tool to guide school district implementation of state standards. Pretty artsy stuff, no? Okay, I know - not the most titillating content! But, as it happens, even that can be approached creatively and with the eye of the artist.

And that's just what we did. Beginning with empathy interviews to be sure that the product we were building was designed for the real people who would be using it and that it was not just an academic exercise. We started small, mining the lived experience of a single person who was struggling, successfully or otherwise, with implementing standards.

Each team interviewed an individual who came from a different background — a teacher on special assignment supporting other teachers, a principal, an assistant superintendent of instruction, and a superintendent. What was there to learn from these individuals' unique experiences that might be a window into a broader truth? What was it in about their stories that might help us tap into something essential that would make our tool a better tool and serve the real needs of people in schools throughout California?

This type of planning and design is more similar to what you might do with a microscope than with a wide-angle lens which might reveal the big picture but loses a lot of granular detail. That kind of approach can lead to overly general solutions.

Empathy interviews have the potential to help you come up with creative, even outlandish ideas, maybe even a flying school bus. And that bus might just take you where you needed to go all along.

chapter nineteen

THE VIEW
FROM HERE

There is a striking sculpture by the renowned artist Richard Serra. The piece, known as Sequence, consists of monumental, sweeping angles of steel. They are so large, in fact, that you can walk inside of its monumental angles and walls. This work of art spent a few years in a large, central gallery that looked out onto Market Street at the San Francisco Museum of Modern Art, where I encountered it.

This piece is massive. It is estimated to weigh 235 tons. Prior to its arrival at SFMOMA, it had most recently resided outdoors at Stanford's Cantor Art Center. Moving it was a logistical feat of some magnitude. Twelve flatbed trucks were required to transport and deliver segments of the piece, right in middle of the bustling downtown traffic of San Francisco. Sequence is powerful in its grandeur; its titanic presence simultaneously elegant and overwhelming.

At an arts colloquium, a museum docent divided me and the other participants into three groups. I sat with my group on blond wood, step-type bleacher seats, perched above the piece. We sketched what we saw from our perch.

Now, drawing has never really been my thing. But when in Rome...

I contemplated Sequence and began to sketch out some rudimentary slopes and angles, capturing, as best I could, the feel of the piece before me. Its gentle grace was easily apparent from the elevated angle from which we viewed the piece.

The ever-intrepid docent interrupted our artmaking and asked us all to leave our clipboards where we sat and come with her to where one of the other groups had been.

"Pick up the clipboard that you find and continue the drawing," she said. I considered the piece before me from this new vantage point, amazed by what I hadn't seen at all from the bench seats. The deep patina of the piece from its recent life outdoors created a rich symphony of oranges and browns, speckled by spots of rust in patterns that seemed crafted by some master painter's hand. I was struck by the depth and beauty of the surface, detail that had blended together to form what appeared to be a uniform brown surface from the distance where I had initially viewed the sculpture.

I picked up the clipboard and tried to add my own impressions to the drawing that the previous viewer had begun (feeling a twinge of guilt that I was somehow sullying my predecessor's stylistic rendering). Then the docent struck again, moving us to a final another location.

Together, my small band of artsy spelunkers journeyed into the middle of the piece, the veritable bowels of the beast. Entering the cavernous curving corridors formed by the steel walls, we landed in a small, rounded "room" created by the curving angular walls of steel towering above us.

It felt oppressive, overwhelming. The immensity of the piece dwarfed us there inside its arms. Looking up at the walls towering over me, I realized that it was all feeling now, not viewing. I picked up the clipboard holding the previous two individuals sketch and added shading here and texture there in my attempt to communicate the feelings evoked in me.

With each successive way of viewing the piece, I had experienced it in a drastically different way. I left that day feeling that I knew this sculpture on a much deeper, more visceral level than when I had when I first glanced at it in the gallery.

I think about that day, sometimes. I was struck by how powerful that piece of art was, viewed from afar, touching and seeing its rich textures close up, and then being engulfed in its immensity and grandeur. They were three visceral and moving experiences, each of them totally distinct and unique — and all in response to what was there all along.

Life is a lot like that. Perceptions shift with location, perspective, and context. The leader's job is to play the role that that docent played — to walk a team to different vantage points, provide them a different way of seeing, and help them build on others' experiences, adding their own unique spin.

Every leader picks up where someone else left off. Sometimes we follow skilled and artful leaders who built beautiful things — and sometimes we follow leaders who have left things fractured, unlovely, and incomplete. It is a leader's job to see the work with fresh eyes from where she stands. Perception is unique, temporary, and contextual — and all the more valuable for it. Deep knowing comes from learning how others perceive things as well.

This is true of art and it is true of systems. In education, experiences look very different depending on where you stand. For example, are you a beneficiary of a privilege that is assigned to you by others based on their assumptions about who you are? Did most of your leaders and teachers look like you — or were they mostly different from you're your experience of school may have been very different based on your answers to those questions. Perhaps you had a pre-charted pathway from elementary school to college where you understood each class, each grade, each experience as a step along that path — or maybe school was new territory for you, and you were left to find your own way through it.

We unwittingly wear blinders that are an artifact of our own internal assumptions, experiences, and beliefs about how we see the world. Humility and self-awareness lead to a very simple idea that changes everything — that everyone's experience is not the same as yours. I know...duh, right? But it is incredibly easy to forget that and make decisions grounded only in our own perspectives, forgetting that there are a universe of different, and equally valid perspectives just outside the door.

There are also times when you need to cut away the excess and noise to get to the heart of the thing. A few years ago, I had the opportunity to tour the studio of Ruth Waters with the artist herself. Ruth is a painter and sculptor who works predominantly in hardwoods, bronze, and marble. Her pieces are lyric and graceful abstract shapes. As she walked me through her studio, she described her work as subtractive. Elaborating, she explained that she uses a mallet and chisel on hardwood and blocks of marble to remove the excess and reveal the shapes and angles that lay hidden in each piece.

Ruth's process is not dissimilar to the work of leaders in systems steeped in tradition and long-standing practice. These leaders must remove layers until the heart of the thing begins to be revealed. Then the real work can begin.

It starts with empathy. It starts with being willing to see and feel the perspective of another in addition to your own.

MORE THAN A MOUSE

Context matters. I have a small painting in my office of Mickey Mouse. To a casual observer, one might think it is just a child's drawing. It is that, but it is also much more to me. A former employee brought it to me the day I was departing a job that I had loved.

She said that she had been talking about my departure at her dinner table and, in the course of the conversation, it came up that I was a fan of Disney. Her preschool-aged, autistic son disappeared into his room. He came out later with a painting that he had created all on his own of Mickey Mouse. It was a gift for me. She was amazed that he had been able to do that on his own and promised him that she would give it to me.

I was struck by this young child's empathy and good-hearted kindness. This young, autistic child somehow knew that his simple act of kindness would matter. And matter it did. That painting holds a place of honor in my office to this day as a symbol of the too oft forgotten trait of empathy that can change everything.

chapter twenty

STRATEGIC LEADERSHIP

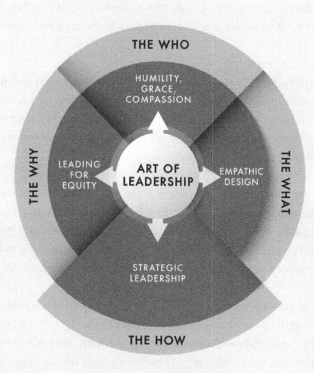

Figure 5.1 Strategic Leadership

When interviewing job applicants, I always ask prospective hires to share a professional mistake and what they learned from it. Over the years, I have heard the gamut of responses. Some give detailed, even tearful, recounts of painful stories of shortcomings and their reckonings.

Recently, a polished and overly-confident applicant said, "Hmmm — Well, I don't believe I have ever made a professional mistake." I regarded her silently for a few moments, waiting for her to elaborate. She did not.

Alrighty then. Although I moved to the next question, it was clear that stellar credentials notwithstanding, there is simply no room in leadership positions for those who have not yet done their own work around self-reflection and humility. Until that happens its not possible to be present for their employees and colleagues in the way that leadership demands of them.

The artful leader is strategic. She begins with the end in mind and moves intentionally and wisely with respect and understanding for people and what motivates them. Artful leaders are learners that integrate the lessons of their successes and — more importantly — their failures into their work.

While it is clear that not everyone is in the same place on their journey of self-reflection, leaders are put to the test every single day — as is their capacity for self-reflection and humility. Unfortunately, such character qualities are not as common as the more popular leadership traits of boldness, rigid adherence to structures, and brash self-confidence.

Strategic leaders know themselves and their systems. They listen and are thoughtful in designing solutions. They hire the right people; people who are smart, collaborative, and humble. Similarly, they don't hire the wrong people, even when project deadlines and workloads create great pressure to do so. Whenever I caved to that kind of pressure and hired the wrong person, I always came to regret it.

This section will detail some of the key strategic skills of the artful leader that form the foundation on which an edifice of change is built.

THE BIG PICTURE

The best leadership is indistinguishable from coaching. It involves being present and aware in those moments when you just don't need another org chart, graph, or table. You need only to be there, and human, in the moment. These are the occasions when life calls you to be humble, to listen, and to offer your presence. It is a mark of the wise leader to heed that call.

At these times, it is good to remember that even though you are grappling with a particularly thorny dilemma that seems overwhelming, it is likely small beans in the grander cosmic opera of life. Today's missed deadline or staff conflict might take on a life of its own, but letting those things distract you from the larger work is a slippery slope. It's also one of those "classes" that life has a way of continuing to sign you up for until you learn it.

In leadership, as in life, most things will go well, but not everything will. You are going to screw up royally sometimes. You will also be brilliant on occasion. Most often, you will have lots of days of being somewhere in-between.

Once I had taken a major promotion and found myself at the helm of a bevy of departments in a division doing high stakes, high profile work. Much of the work was new to me, and the staff was counting on me to support them. Fortuitously, I happened across a verse that Ralph Waldo

Emerson reportedly wrote to his daughter, Ellen, in 1854. Its wisdom resonated with me in that moment. It is still on my desk today, the paper it is written on a bit worn and stained by the years:

> "Finish each day and be done with it. You have done what you could. Some blunders and absurdities no doubt crept in; forget them as soon as you can. Tomorrow is a new day. You shall begin it serenely and with too high a spirit to be encumbered with your old nonsense."

Always find the light and move towards it. No, I'm not talking about the proverbial light at the end of the tunnel. You'll get to that one soon enough! I'm talking about that light that warms things; the light of compassion, patience, persistence, and humility. That one.

You will have days that will suck. There will be days when shitty things happen to you — days when you make the wrong choice and live to regret it. There will be days when people you trusted the most will let you down when it really matters. I've had all of those days. I know you have, too.

Don't let them deter you from the steady march toward what matters. In your weakest and most desperate moment, give the last of what you have to someone else. It doesn't matter if they need it — or deserve it — or will take advantage. Do it anyway.

It's a fair argument for leadership as well as life. There will always be plenty of reasons to mistrust people. As a leader you will surely see both the heights as well as the depths of human capacity and self-interest.

But you will also see more, if you take the time to look.

More importantly, how you conduct yourself in leadership will either inspire others to greatness or push them to self-interest and arrogance. Be bold. Be courageous. Do good work that matters to those who can never repay you and for whom there is no rationale other than it is the right thing to do.

THE CASE FOR SQUARE PEGS

One of the most important functions of the leader is hiring the right people. This is very much a part of strategic leadership. Hire the right people, and amazing things will happen. Hire the wrong ones, and you will spend many difficult days managing conflicts, countering missed opportunities, and handling the myriad avoidable challenges that came with having the wrong people on the bus.

You might think I am referring to hiring Rhodes scholars, valedictorians, and Mensa members. I'm not. Now, don't get me wrong, smart people can rock your organization in good ways. But there are also other traits that I have learned make teams function operate efficiently and to coalesce.

I have hired hundreds of people in my career, and I have found a few tried and true measures of what makes a person outstanding. First, hire smart people who have a bent toward coloring outside the lines. There are some very smart people who are so wedded to routine that they can't innovate. Truth, it generally turns out, resides in the multi-hued shades of grey that define the work that we do and the world we live in.

Build teams of people who get that. Hire those who listen deeply, innovate relentlessly, and who will question you and your assumptions. Pay attention to those who think outside the proverbial box and shake things up. They will cause you no end of grief — and you will be better off for it.

I once worked for a particularly wise and empathic leader who wanted to figure out the secret sauce to hiring the best people. He wanted to understand the difference in the organization's heroes and superstars versus those who were consistently unsuccessful, despite all interventions to assist them. So, he had both sets of these people interviewed about their thoughts, attitudes, and beliefs in the interest of ferreting out what internal factors contributed to success or failure in the workplace.

Surprisingly, he found two things. The highfliers were self-reflective, sometimes even totally unsure if the path they were on was the right one. They were constantly making course adjustments. Ironically, those who were not performing well tended to be more certain and self-confident and saw their work in terms of black and white, good and bad.

Secondly, and an unexpected outcome, the highest performers consistently had a sense of humor and lightness about their work. These individuals approached challenges that they faced with ease and playfulness. They defused situations with humor and had a "Take it all in stride" way of being that prompted them not to sweat the small stuff. In contrast, those who struggled tended to be dead serious about how things should be. They had hard and fast rules about how they believed things were supposed to work.

This wise leader incorporated these lenses into hiring procedures. As a consequence, he assembled a team that collaborated and developed a remarkable track record of innovation, collaboration, and positive morale.

One of the key traits that make exceptional leaders is humility — that deep understanding that all people have unique experiences and others' lived experiences are no less valid than their own.

Build a team of *relentless collaborators.* No, really. I don't mean the type of collaboration that I observed in a former co-worker who used the language of collaboration, inviting everyone to "collaborate" around to her idea. If they had alternate ideas, she was quick to dismiss them out of hand.

Really collaborate. Listen, share, be unnerved, risk failure, and share the ownership of tasks. You — and your organization — will be better for it.

I realized in my very first principalship that it was a far better use of my time to create work environments where the best people wanted to work (it was also much more rewarding...and enjoyable). Rather than spend my energies constantly recruiting new people or dealing with the fallout from those that weren't a fit, I found myself able to attract good people by making an inviting and professionally invigorating place to work.

I learned a few things about the kinds of places where the best people wanted to work. They were, I realized, the kinds of places where I wanted to work, too. They were places where you had some autonomy and weren't forced to spend precious mental energy and time on things that didn't matter. They were places where you had freedom to create, innovate, and collaborate. They were environments where failure was a marker that you were trying hard enough and lack of at least some failure meant you were playing too much in the safe zone.

It is worth noting that while money is surely an important motivator, it is not the most compelling thing to keep people inspired to do their best work. Creating working conditions that attract, sustain, and build strong employees is always time well spent.

The success of a leader is largely an artifact of the quality and caliber of staff that she builds. Hire the right people, know what to be tight about (outcomes), and what to be loose with (strategies to get to those outcomes), and let your people fly. When you hire staff who are inspired and inspiring, self-reflective, and who have a clear "why" to their work that aligns with yours and the organization's, there is no limit to what you will accomplish.

chapter twenty-one

OF LIFE AND LEADERSHIP

Greta was a young manager who worked for me in a number of increasingly responsible roles. At one point, when she was a mid-level manager and direct contributor, I invited her to sit in as an interview panelist searching for the perfect candidate for a high profile, high stakes position. The interviewee was to be the director of a signature initiative of the organization.

Greta was about to go out on maternity leave, so her days in the office were numbered. Nevertheless, I valued her skill, sharp insights, and forward-thinking ways. I knew that she would have the right insight to help assess applicants. She was eloquent, a deep thinker, and had a bold vision that was not limited by the reality and confines of the work as it currently existed. People loved working with her, and she had an uncanny ability to inspire enthusiasm and creativity.

Pondering the latest in a series of panels of candidates, I was chagrined. None of them were what I was looking for with the right blend of vision, savvy, and skill for this very public initiative. I remember waking up one morning at 3:00 a.m., having gone to sleep frustrated with this latest set of candidates. Twisting and turning, I struggled for the answer.

"I need," I thought to myself, "someone like Greta."

In a moment of psychic "Duh," I realized that I didn't want someone like Greta; I wanted Greta! The solution had been right in front of my face all along.

Some weeks later, when Greta was able to slip out of her house for a few minutes during the new baby's nap time, we met for coffee near her home. As we sipped our coffee, I explained my thinking to her, my vision for this new initiative, and how I would like her to take the helm of this new team. I promised that I would hold the position open for her until she was ready to return to work.

Greta took the new role and executed it masterfully, never compromising her dynamic vision, while building a smart, collaborative, and high-functioning team that led innovative work and launched a host of dynamic partnerships that continue to this day.

Greta exemplified artful leadership. She was driven by a passion for social justice and approached her leadership in a manner that was both playful and rigorous. She was a skilled facilitator and student of intentional design. In a variety of ways, Greta, to my mind, is an archetype for artful leadership in its nuance, focus, humanity, and grace. Over time, she built a team culture of innovation and collaboration. Never content with the status quo, her team built new programs and systems that achieved remarkable results.

A few years into her new role, it was with a mixture of understanding and disappointment that I accepted Greta's resignation. By this time, she had two young daughters at home, neither of whom was in school yet. She had decided to take a year off to spend time with them in their final year before beginning school.

Sometimes has other plans, though. It was only a few short weeks into this planned kiddo sabbatical that Greta's older daughter, Elsie, became ill and just couldn't shake it. A routine visit to the doctor turned into a battery of tests and anxiety that culminated in Greta and her husband receiving news that would forever change their lives. Four year old Elsie was diagnosed with leukemia.

There are moments when life calls on us to summon our best, most courageous selves. Greta faced her moment with grace and resolve. She brought the same ways of being to this new "normal" of her life that she had relied upon in her leadership.

Greta and her husband began blogging their journey with Elsie through the hard days of treatment, chronicling their journey while providing friends and family a way to stay connected to young Elsie's progress. With her best, focused, and empathic self at the forefront, Greta told their story with honesty, grace, and, where she could find it, good humor.

Hers was a tale of painful treatments, steroids, and the reactions to the Dexamethasone corticosteroid treatment that transformed little Elsie from their silly, playful little girl to someone who was under the influence of what they would come came to call the Decamonster. Her journey through the challenges of life with this new reality that none of them could have anticipated was both inspiring and moving.

It included supporting Elsie's little sister, Ani, who didn't quite understand why life had changed so much overnight. In fact, under Greta and her husband's parental leadership, Ani came to be a stellar model of a little sister. Their story is filled with highs and lows, angst and fear, tantrums and triumphs.

I share Greta's story as an exemplar that the ways of being that make a remarkable leader also make for a remarkable life. Greta's journey exemplified grace, compassion, and artistry, though I'm sure from their perspective she was just doing the very best that they could to get through each day and be as ready as they possibly could be for what the next one held.

The journey was one of gritty grace, resilience, and community. Recently, I had the good fortune to attend young Elsie's fifth birthday party and "Cancerversary" in Golden Gate Park in San Francisco. We wore gold to celebrate her progress and imminent entry into kindergarten, a normal and ordinary thing that, like so many such things these days, could no longer taken for granted. Each normal life event had new meaning and was infused with gratitude and wonder.

It turns out that there is a simple grace to living (and leading), and the two are not unrelated at all. What is more, I also learned that a five-year-old warrior can teach us all a lot about passion, purpose, and grit as she leads her life fighting a battle few of us will ever see let alone experience.

Look for those who live life well and courageously, no matter what life hands them. They are the kind of people a leader should want to hire, and they are the kind of people who are capable of great leadership.

I've always been drawn to people who are scrappy, ingenious, ballsy, or just plain wise. You know the type: those people who have faced some stuff and tend to know things that the rest of us don't. They are people who don't settle, who push themselves to be better, and — as leaders — who inspire and push (or sometimes pull) others to be better, too. Particularly when hiring people to work in schools, I found time and again that those who have overcome some personal challenge or difficulty in life have a deeper sense of empathy.

As with most things in life and leadership, you have a basic choice to make. You can take the path of least resistance — do the easy thing, don't ruffle feathers, and stay off the limbs that more courageous people congregate on. Or you can say "Screw it" and do all of those things. Go for broke, take a position, speak truth to power, and call them like you see them. I prefer the latter path.

TEACHABLE MOMENTS

One morning recently, I stopped by a colleague's office and he recounted the prior day's staff retreat. The meeting agenda was tossed out in favor of deep conversation around the "why" of the work of his team. It was an unanticipated conversation that emerged authentically, and he was wise enough to let it happen.

He saw the opportunity in that moment for his team to better understand their collective purpose. He knew instinctively the value in the team understanding a higher purpose to the work to which they devoted countless hours, energy, and sweat. He understood that if they got it, they could change the conditions of life and learning for children. He also knew that the team had struggled with agreeing on shared definitions and that there was value in leaning in on this teachable moment. A wise leader seizes those moments when they find them.

It takes some wisdom and bravery in being comfortable in discomfort. This leader understood inherently that this messy and emotional process for his team was the work — and that everything that emerged from that wellspring would be richer and better. It is in those moments of brilliance where true leadership emerges.

What motivates people to do their best work? It is inspiring when that flow and energy manifests. When people find the inspiration and give

120 percent, working tirelessly or, more accurately, getting quite tired but keep going forward anyway, fantastic things can happen. What is it that sets the stage for these conditions to occur?

Sure, part of it has to do with the type of people that you have on a team - people with passion, commitment, and drive. But there ways for a leader to set the right conditions in which this type of energy, passion, and innovation to grow among any set of people.

I have learned that a lot of it has to do with motivation. When leaders trust, support, and give space and resources to people, the conditions are created in which the type of work that changes systems can occur. Artful leaders build skills to support and respect their teams. They listen. They are there to cheer their teams on when they are successful and pick them up and dust them off when they stumble.

But just as leaders can create the right conditions for these things to flourish, they can just as easily poison the environment. They can turn a team's motivation from a focus on achieving outcomes to that of covering their own backsides. All it takes for a leader to change what a staff is focused on from outcomes to self-protection is an environment in which workers are not trusted, are micro-managed, and are punished in one form or another, implicit or explicit, for mistakes. These are the kinds of trust that, once broken, takes a long time and concerted effort to heal.

A lot of leadership qualities come from the kind of person the leader is and the life he or she leads. Is a person's leadership focused on others and good outcomes — or is it focused on self and ego? The answer to that question is a key to success in both leadership and life.

chapter twenty-two

GOOD ENOUGH CHICKEN

The elected county superintendent job comes with the following perks: impossible hours juggling a large governmental organization; interacting with other elected and community leaders; serving as the voice of education in the county; supervising a large workforce, managing countywide crises that invariably occur, overseeing complex budgets, and navigating the dynamic needs of multiple school districts, to name just a few. All this is expected in addition to being present to represent the office at an endless stream of community events.

A recently retired county superintendent shared that in the midst of managing this kind of schedule, she and her husband had developed a fallback plan for dinner, when neither of them really had time to plan and execute a grand culinary experience. They would make plain chicken breasts and possibly accompany it with some rice. Nothing exciting, no Zagat rating in the wings, but it got the job done.

"We call it 'good enough chicken,'" she told me.

Not too long ago, I ran for elected office. I learned many lessons through this process. One lesson was to forego perfectionism when the demands are intense. I learned to ensure high quality work but let go of the need for perfection. In short, I learned the concept of "good enough chicken."

I was blessed along the way to work with some remarkable people, such as a former, highly respected superintendent who had formerly held the post for which I was running. She was at once my champion, partner-in-crime, and truth-teller. There were days, over the course of the campaign, when I would enjoy some of those things more than others. It was hard when she would do the critical, often thankless work of providing the unvarnished truth. Yet I came to respect her throughout for her intelligence, generosity, tenacity, and work ethic. Sometimes in our lives we meet people who remind us what it is to be our very best version of ourselves.

The campaign would become a 24-month under-taking, filled with hundreds of coffees, fund-raisers, press releases, and debates. A mountain of endorsements would come from local and national elected officials, teachers, labor unions, community leaders, and staff of the office that I would be leading. Our message was a simple one — we wanted a County Office of Education led with integrity and a focus on serving all children and youth, and a commitment to educating the whole child.

It was a message that would resonate with many people including quite literally hundreds of community leaders who enthusiastically shared the vision. It resonated, in fact, with 49.5% of the voters, but, as fate would have it, failed to land with 50.5% of them.

It was an unexpected and hard-felt loss and it hurt, particularly because of the enthusiasm and passion of those who had stood with me and the loss of the opportunity for our shared vision for children and youth to become a reality.

Working full-time while running a full-time campaign was no joke. My campaign manager/former superintendent and I spoke the same language and shared a penchant for perfectionism. She had learned a few things in her time around the block, though. I remember early on in the campaign when I was sweating over some detail — the perfect type font, photo selection for campaign materials (this picture of these three kids, that one of those two, or the other one of three others entirely), or exactly which shade of blue in the logo really defined me — she told me the story that was to become a principle of the campaign: her "good enough chicken" story.

Over the course of the intense, sometimes maddening campaign that we would run, it became our code for when we had spent enough on things, the input received had been vetted and considered, and various permutations bandied about. Sometimes we had to settle for "Good enough chicken."

It meant that while it could most surely be better, it was good and we'd be fine with having it go out to the public. It was time for us to move on to other pressing matters waiting in the wings for our attention. It meant we were accepting it with a few imperfections (though no typos or grammatical errors; those neither of us could abide), but the rest was good — or good enough. Good enough chicken.

Managing the workflow while ensuring that the preponderance of time is spent on things that matter most is a critical skill for leaders. It is a necessary step in strategizing and accomplishing goals.

I have always had bold ambitions, never content to just get by. I pretty much come to the party wanting to do things ten times better than the next guy. While that is just how I am put together, I have learned that sometimes there is deep wisdom in remembering the principle of "good enough chicken." It is otherwise too easy to start down the slippery slope of overly focusing on the details and losing sight of the big picture. Developing a sense of what to let go of and what to maintain a tight hold on is part of the Great Balancing Act of the skillful leader.

chapter twenty-three

HUMILITY, GRACE, & COMPASSION

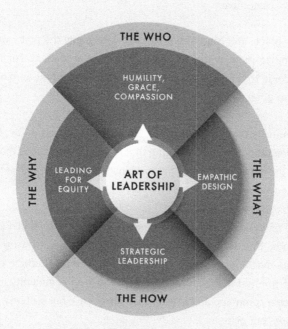

Figure 6.1, Humility, Grace, and Compassion.

S ometimes we find shared ways that we are reminded of the tenacity and grit that undergird kindness and compassion. When U.S. Congressman and civil rights icon Elijah Cummings passed away in 2019, there was national mourning for this remarkable share-cropper's son turned United States Congressman and the chasm that his death left in our collective consciousness as a people.

It was perhaps former President Barack Obama who said it best, speaking at Congressman Cummings's funeral:

> "There's nothing weak about kindness and com-
> passion. There's nothing weak about looking out
> for others. There's nothing weak about being
> honorable."

Humility, grace, and compassion are not necessarily the first words that may come to mind when you think about great leaders. Far too few leaders come to the work of with those skills coming first to mind when describing great leadership.

In fact, humility may be the most under-appreciated trait of the leader. It is not overstating the case to argue that it is the secret sauce that differentiates the great leader from the marginally competent, self-serving, or even failed leader.

Meg Wheatley is a writer and key thinker on leadership, social systems, and change. She describes systems as being more akin to living ecosystems than machines — think more rainforest and less turbine engine. I think she got that right. She argues for a focus on community and connection over command and control if we are to save our systems, and, for that matter, our planet.

Plenty of leaders still wittingly or unwittingly ascribe to the traditional factory-based models of systems. Most often, this leads to results that range from the disappointing to the disastrous.

Humility, as it happens, is not a thing that traditional canons of leadership have historically opined on. But in it lies the heart of the artful leader. She is humble enough to see the system and the people within it as a living ecosystem, all essential to the well-being of the whole, rather than replaceable cogs in a machine.

Humility comes with a predilection for listening. It can't be emphasized enough that the best leaders tend to be the best listeners. They get the importance of having smarter people working for them, who question their own assumptions and embrace change.

Now, don't get me wrong. Even the most humble leader who is skilled in facilitating and listening, will eventually have to move a project forward, to hold staff accountable, and execute. I remember clearly a quite innovative initiative that I worked on called the "iZone" when I was a Deputy Superintendent. It had a winning mix of smart people, generative spaces, and a collective impact model that leveraged leaders and thinkers from multiple sectors, all working in concert. To be fair, some quality work came out of the project. But the larger work was also hampered by a failure to differentiate between the time for generating ideas and brainstorming versus the time to shift to focused implementation. High impact initiatives manage to straddle both of those things.

Good implementation plans circle back to evaluate and gather additional data, but groups can become fatigued with putting their best thinking and energies into a plan, only to continually revisit it and develop an alternate plan at the next meeting... and the next... and the next. Humility and self-reflection paired with focus and a commitment to design, create a powerful leadership combination.

The thing about humble leadership is that it is not some secondary, nice-to-have soft skill. It is a hard choice to make, in fact, to live and lead in a space of inquiry and humility. The ability to consider multiple perspectives creates the conditions for powerful work to occur. Suffice it to say that this is not always easy. It takes an investment of time and some discipline to stop, listen, and consider multiple points of view when things are moving at the speed of light. But, boy, is it ever worth it.

In my years as a school counselor, I worked at the elementary, middle, and high school levels counseling students through whatever challenges or crises they faced. I also consulted with teachers and administrators around how to best serve students. Truth is, early on I didn't always understand how the work I did as a counselor had anything much to do with leadership. I was to learn that it had just about everything to do with it.

My work as a counselor served as a lab to hone the skills of listening. What I experienced sitting across from students in individual and group counseling settings changed me and how I understand schools and systems more broadly. There is something rare and special about students sharing their truth about their lives — the highs and, more often, the lows.

It would be a lesson that I cemented during a few years that I served as a foster parent for adolescents with behavioral and emotional disabilities. These young people had lived lives that no child should ever have to live and had developed elaborate coping skills as a response to the trauma of their lives. While it would have been easy to just respond to their acting out behaviors, employing enough empathy to understand where these behaviors came from and how they had been necessary to their survival shifted the conversation and focus and made healing possible.

SUPERPOWERS

When I would make the switch into my first leadership role in the years ahead, I mistakenly believed, at first, that those lessons were ones that I needed to put behind me to be a strong leader. It was time to be bold, direct, courageous, and confident — a superhero, cape and all. Oh, geez!

I learned (thankfully, in short order) that that was a bunch of hogwash. Don't get me wrong. Some of those things surely have a place in our leadership playbook on occasion, but most of them are more about ego and fear of things falling apart than they are about leadership. In fact, I would come to learn that the most powerful skills of the leader are those of the counselor — listening, empathy, and shared problem-solving.

I have learned a lot observing visionary and inspiring leaders as well as small-minded and inconsequential ones. You don't have to look far to find evidence that bravado without conscience, bluster without substance, and confidence without compassion are destructive.

The way of the artful leader is about different things — things like humility, listening, collaborative design, and empathy. They have informed me about the lived experience of others, even those with whom I disagree. While they may have produced longer decision-making process, there is no doubt that they have also produced better ones. Decisions are deeper and more nuanced when they are informed by the perspective of those that they impact.

Perhaps you are someone who sees the need for change in our public systems, I do too. This isn't leadership for incrementalism. It takes strong, bold action that has been informed by reflection, empathy, and shared design.

It is a tragedy of our times that compassion, kindness, and collaboration have become synonymous with weakness. We live in fractured times, and it is easy for leaders to adopt a strident mentality. In fact, our leaders need to have backbones of steel these days to stand up to the some-times daily assaults on our values. But maybe that is the wrong met-aphor. Steel, while strong, can shatter if sufficient pressure is exerted. I suspect the engineer would suggest to us that a more malleable and pliable substance would better stand the application of extreme pres-sure. A substance that, while strong, could bend and yet continue to have internal integrity and be resolute. The same is true for leaders.

Being strong and unyielding is a tool that every leader must have in his or her toolkit to be used, for example, when a collaborative and ethical solution is being implemented and facing assaults from without. Yet far too many leaders begin with that frame of reference and have nowhere to go when their immovable object faces immense pressure.

While the strong, charismatic, and unyielding leader can attract some attention and following, their effectiveness only persists to their breaking point. Their solutions, their policies, are truly only as resilient as the extent to which they address their followers' and clients' true needs. Absent the humility that comes with compromise and shared meaning-making, their shelf life is limited.

The artful leader stands on the ground of humility, grace, and compas-sion. They regularly practice the art of active listening. They consider multiple opinions and points of view. They lean in towards empathy and understand the perspectives of those whom their work will impact. They understand the importance in supervision that pauses the mad pace, even for a few minutes, in order to be present when an employee, a cli-ent, or colleague needs to be heard. They are able to move in and out of this stance smoothly.

Humility, grace, and compassion are the simplest, and simultaneously the most complex, of the traits of the artful leader. And they are the traits that most transform leadership.

chapter twenty-four

THE FINE ART OF LOSS

There are a few remarkable people you encounter in life. Jackie Speier is one of those people for me. She has long been a fighter for those without a voice. She is a wise and courageous US Congresswoman for California's 14th congressional district — and she is nobody's fool. She has consistently been a staunch champion in the fight for women's rights, LGBTQ rights, and for the disenfranchised.

Jackie is no stranger to overcoming obstacles. Early in her career, as a 28-year-old aide to then Congressman Leo Ryan, she joined the congressman on a visit to Jonestown on a fact-finding mission to Jim Jones's Peoples Temple compound. Returning to the airstrip with several defectors, Jones gunmen ambushed the group, killing Congressman Ryan and several others. The news reports tell that Jackie was left lying nearly lifeless after being shot five times at point blank range with an assault rifle.

Congresswoman Speier has been quoted as saying that she had a choice to make in that moment: Did she want to be a victim or be a fighter? She chose the latter, a decision that she says propelled her into the life she was meant to live. It has been a life of great consequence that has left the world a better place.

It has always struck me that learning and success are tethered to our relationship with failure and loss. I will cop to having spouted lofty platitudes to adolescents when I worked with them as a counselor back in the day about failure being an essential part of learning. I actually believe that. There is something transformative about taking life's misses, failures, and (even) stunning defeats in stride and not letting them floor you. The theory says to learn from them and try again — getting better and wiser each time.

It is a hell of a good theory.

But life, as it will do, had some lessons in store for me.

When I ran for public office, I spent the better part of two years putting in exhaustively long hours, expending passion, money, and summoning all of the courage I could to run my political campaign. It was invigorating because I so believed in my mission and the work that lay ahead and how it could change the lives of children. Running for office was something I never thought that I would do, particularly not as an openly gay candidate. Growing as a gay kid in the South with all of the angst and cognitive dissonance that came along with that, "coming out" to countless community leaders and speaking publicly about my journey was unsettling and uncertain at first. I would come to find out, though, as many before me and since have, that owning who I was in an authentic and unapologetic way was liberating for me in ways that I could not have anticipated.

Ok, so as not to bury the lead, this particular story didn't have a happy ending. It was, however, a critical time in my understanding of public policy, loyalty, and ethics. The race was one that I had planned for years. In fact, I had told my boss, who held the post I would run for, eight years prior that I would never run against her but would do so when she was ready to retire.

I was incredibly humbled to have near universal, enthusiastic support from the staff who would be working for me and who knew both me and my opponent well. Similarly, I was supported by the vast majority of the governing board and almost every local, state, and federal elected official in the county as well as teachers from across the county. It was an amazing rallying of those who shared a vision with me for students and how we could change the equation for them.

Somewhere along the course of the campaign, a former employee of mine decided to run against me. I won't go into the more Machiavellian machinations of the campaign that I experienced, but suffice it to say that I made a decision, early on, to be true to myself and come out on the other end, win or lose, with my ethics intact and able to look at myself in the mirror. While it turns out that that may be winning strategy for living an ethical life, it is not so much one for winning a political race.

On election night, with tens of thousands of votes counted, I had won by a slight margin. However, it was the county's first all-mail ballots election, which meant that ballots would continue to come in for weeks. As each successive report came out, the count danced around either side of the fifty percent mark. One day I would be ahead; the next my opponent would be.

In the end, as I've mentioned, in the final tally I lost by one-half of a percent. Not only did the realization of this loss hit me as any political loss would. It was a double whammy because I worked as deputy to the elected official, who was the person to whom I had just lost. Thus, my beloved job that I was so passionate about was also gone. Kaput.

One of the most bitter pills to swallow was the undoing of much of the work I had done over the past twelve years. Many people who had supported me in those endeavors left their jobs, either because they didn't believe in the direction the office was headed or felt pushed out. The trail of devastation from this loss is one that I would feel for months. It was my own lesson about what it means to risk greatly...and lose.

I had put it all on the line — my job, my resources, and the good will and generosity of countless friends and supporters.

The campaign was a proving field for me in courage, humility, and self-awareness. The experience was at times thrilling, excruciating, inspiring, and maddening. And it was mine — not only to live, but to make sense of. It was a walk, for all its difficulty, that taught me much about myself and how our political structures work — and, coincidentally, quite a bit about leadership.

The day that the final count came in and I knew that I had lost the election, I was sitting alone in a hotel room in Anaheim, California. I was at Disneyland, ironically, the happiest place on earth. Yeh, that day, not so much. I was attending an educational arts conference and went upstairs to my room to await the final reporting. In the preceding weeks, I had seen my lead increase, seen it slip away, and — on this sunny afternoon, I would learn that I had lost.

I was exhausted. It was a shocker, to be sure. The work had been seemingly endless. The long days and nights of worry had all given way to this moment. Losing was a bitter pill. I received a call from a political consultant who had worked with the campaign as well as from some of my closest and most engaged followers, friends, and colleagues. This was a blip. Better things were in store, they said. Everyone was in shock. You get the idea

Much as I had counseled so many middle school students years earlier, I told myself that the task was not to wallow in loss, but to learn from it and build on the opportunities that losing afforded me. In all fairness, I didn't want to hear that advice. Not then.

In short order, I would be fortunate to find another job in my field that I loved. I would help, however I could, supporters who were displaced to find a place to land. I was left with making sense of this moment in the broader story of my life.

The stakes had been high and what might have been was not going to be. I was haunted by a memory of a film I had seen years earlier about a high school athlete who had lost his championship game and lived the rest of his life in a space of loss and regret for what might have been.

"Oh, hell no," I told myself. "I am not going to be that guy."

Sometimes life signs you up for life lessons you never really wanted. It's kind of like that really impossible college math or language course that you didn't really want to take, but you had to get through to get to the cool courses in your major.

Leadership and life like are filled with a hodgepodge of ups and downs. I really prefer the "ups" if I'm being straight with you, thank you very much. But the truth is that making something of those "downs" defines who you are as a leader and — more importantly — as a person.

Early on in the process, a wise and beloved former local state assembly-man, Rich Gordon, gave me some good advice: "Don't let the process change you," he counseled. "Be true to who you are and be able to look at yourself in the mirror after it's over." It was advice that I would try to hold closely to through the white-water rapids of the campaign.

There were moments too, moments filled with meaning and in no way diminished by the outcome of the race. One of these was when I received the endorsement of local U.S. Congresswoman, Jackie Speier. Having been an ardent admirer of hers, I was honored beyond words to have her support for my campaign as well as her endorsement, let alone her beautiful consolation when it was all over. She wrote to me:

> "It is not the defeat that marks a candidate. It is the success that they can identify even in defeat. Please mark yourself as highly worthy in the eyes of the community because you ran a good race, stuck to the facts, and avoided actions that would reflect poorly on yourself and others, and you addressed the top concerns of the electorate. In victory or defeat we serve as civic educators. You thought that you'd earned your Ph.D. before this election. Now, you should realize that you may claim a second Ph.D. - in civic virtue - and this one was earned with high honors.
>
> All the best,
> Jackie Speier"

The campaign, filled with such shining moments, was an experience that changed me, as the best experiences, even the crappy ones, often do. Sometimes it is indeed what we learn about life and ourselves, even in defeat, that makes the difference.

Every leader will face his or her challenges, both large and small. It is not the absence of these that reveals one's mettle; it is, instead, what you make of them. Turns out, the advice that I had given those middle school-ers so many years prior was true, though the journey through failure is not an easy one. It calls on each of us as leader to find our center and stay oriented, always, towards the light.

chapter twenty-five

TURN THE LIGHTS ON

I am, almost always, the first one into my office. In fact, I am more often than not the first one pretty much anywhere I go. It's just how I'm wired. Anyone who knows me is either horribly annoyed or exceedingly grateful about this: mostly the former in my personal life, and the latter professionally.

I think it is something I learned from my dad. "If you're on time, you're late," was his motto. My mother used to say that we were always the first ones to every event we attended.

I recall the rehearsal in the afternoon prior to commencement ceremonies when I earned my doctorate. It was the afternoon rehearsal for the early evening commencement ceremonies. There, far in the distant bleachers, were two figures. I knew it was my mom and dad. They were there, in their seats, ready for the ceremonies that would not begin for hours.

The corollary to this relationship with time and arrivals was that we most often always left things early, too, to be the first ones out of the parking lot as my dad said, to beat the traffic. So while I saw lots of amazing things in my childhood, I really don't know how any of them ended.

In my current schedule, I have a long commute, which is rather new, so you would think I would have backed my schedule up and hauled into the office a little later. Not so much. My penchant to be early is hardwired in.

There is something about being the first one in and turning on the lights that I like. It is a feeling of a new day starting. There are some hope and promise tied up around that; hope about what is possible.

I like turning on lights and illuminating dark places, literally and figuratively. There is just something powerful about shedding light on a thing. There are days when I have been on a beach, or a mountain, or sitting in a cafe in the late afternoon when the slant of light was just right — a golden, somehow holy, glow of light — that is remarkable. It changes everything it touches and allows you to see the same things differently. I'm reminded, in those moments, that so much in life is about perspective.

Yet, as much as I love the light, life isn't always lit with that golden, warm glow. Sometimes its light is overcast and filtered through crappy dark clouds. Sometimes you can barely find your way in the dimming light, while at other times the light blinds you and makes the everything appear in silhouette. Sometimes the light is so harsh that it nearly blinds you - like when you're driving down the interstate and have to hold your hand up to block the glare. Light can be fickle.

When I think about it, much of what I have learned about leadership is illuminating dark places, bringing into the open what was there all along, and sometimes lighting it in a way so you see something familiar in an entirely new way.

When I was a geeky drama major getting my undergrad more years ago than I care to mention, I loved the stage but always had an affinity for the techies. They were the people who were creative but not in an artsy-fartsy, emo, dramatic way. They were the lighting designers, set designers, prop masters, and stage managers. They seemed to have baked into their nature a wry sense of humor, a biting sarcastic streak, and oddly anti-artsy (okay, and sometimes anti-social) personality traits.

Case in point: I had a good friend named Lynn. Lynn was a no nonsense blond badass bitch who wore overalls and pretty much said whatever was on her mind. She had a vocabulary that ran from blunt to salty. I always suspected from the slight curve of the corner of her lips when she said something particularly unpopular that she liked inhabiting that social space that others avoided.

Lynn had an affinity for lighting design, a craft at which she excelled. We spent many hours together, during those years, in the theatre. Lynn was famous for her frustration with actors who were oblivious to her intricate lighting designs and wandered to some darkened corner of the stage to deliver their great dramatic moment rather than hit their marks. There it was — the light prepared and gelled properly, the cue coming up at just the right moment to invoke the desired mood, and the actor was standing three feet away in the dark. Lynn, for her part, was not amused. She would yell (or, more accurately, bellow at times), during tech rehearsals. You could hear her from the catwalk above or the control booth: "Find your fucking light!" It became something of a joke or a tagline for how we thought of Lynn.

Funny how life is so often like that. Everything we worked and planned for is coming together — and we fall short in covering that last ten feet of pipe, as they say, and stepping into the light.

Sometimes we need a Lynn to remind us to find our light — especially when we get stuck in the darkness that life inevitably deals us — or in the fog and filtered light of compromise and doubt and jealously.

My advice to you, in the immortal words of my old friend Lynn, is to find your *fucking light*. It's there, I have discovered. You just have to trust it and be courageous enough to step into it.

There is a thing about the quality of light. Stage lighting designers know this. Photographers know this. Anyone who has walked on a beach at sunset knows this.

At the risk of waxing overly poetic, live your life (and situate your leadership) in the light. The artful leader orients herself towards the light. I have worked for and with countless leaders. The best among them have been motivated by and moved systems toward the light — toward the well-being of children, creating a more equitable world, calling out injustice, and nurturing creativity.

Most of these things were less about them than about the purpose of their work and the unique "light" that they found in it. But I have worked for other leaders too, those who have been motivated by personal self-interest, fear, or questionable agendas. Their leadership has been without purpose and has done far more harm than good and was a waste of time and energy and passion. These types of leaders really, really need to find their light because far too many stumble around in the darkness breaking things.

Artful leaders illuminate dark places. Often that means looking at things — systems, people, or situations — openly and honestly, even when it is hard to do so. Sometimes it means being willing to call out hypocrisy and injustice where you see it and stand willing to bear the consequences of that. Sometimes it means staying aware that there are perspectives, information, or thoughts that are outside the field of vision of the leader.

Good leaders are also focused. Some years ago, I worked for a woman who was a strong leader. The organization was closing down a decades old program, an educational resource center. It was a hard thing, really. The center, once vibrant, had shown years of declining use as the field shifted to new online sources for their materials and information. Ironically, the initiative was where the organization's current leader had begun her career and it was near and dear to her heart.

In time, the relevant issues had been thoroughly explored, input had been sought, and a careful decision-making process had concluded that it was time to close this initiative to allow the resources to support other initiatives. When it was time to begin the multi-month process to close the program, there were a host of hurdles, concerns, and push-back. I witnessed the leader's quiet, focused tenacity in implementing the decision at hand without getting distracted by the incoming shrapnel.

This is an essential skill for the leader, though it is one that must be deployed thoughtfully. Had this leader applied her tenacity to a solution that had not been thoughtfully developed, it would have been an organizational nightmare. The wise leader needs to be nimble (and wise) in shifting from a facilitative, design stance to the implementation mode and then back out again when it is time to evaluate and adjust course.

THE THING ABOUT TRUST

Artful leaders who are in the business of shining light must also develop the skill of inviting others to see things in new ways. The kind of relationship required to have these types of coaching and supervision conversations is built on trust.

Trust, in fact, is the coin of the realm for the leader. It is one of those things that takes time to build but can be destroyed in a single incident. When it is built, it is the foundation for amazing work that happens more fluidly, easily, and quickly. I have learned how important it is to be genuine and honest with employees and employers alike. That matters immensely.

An aspiring leader that I was recently coaching asked me to help her to understand this thing called transparency. She was perplexed about how a leader makes decisions, seeks input, remains open, but doesn't violate confidentiality or share information that they are not at liberty to disclose. It was, to her, a conundrum.

Our ensuing conversation was about trust, how leaders build and some- times break it. The young leader in question had recently received a pro- motion that would result in her supervising former colleagues — a situa- tion that was causing her some stress as she prepared for her new role.

She was a smart go-getter. In fact, she had already made some deci- sions about how to increase organizational efficiency and had shared some of her new systems with her former colleagues/new reports. She had been greeted with a steely response to her request for feedback: "Management is going to do whatever they want to," they replied to her. "What does it matter what we think?"

As we talked, she came to the realization that building a relationship with her new team through empathy and learning about their thoughts, experiences, and perspectives were necessary precursors to the kind of programmatic shifts she was proposing. Transparency, she reflected in a moment of "a-ha," was about authenticity, openness, and positive intent rather than about simply telling people what you have decided.

When a leader acts out of some hidden agenda, it is apparent at one-hun- dred paces. When that happens, the focus of attention shifts from doing the work to managing the relationship. Trust plays an absolutely critical role in the daily life of the artful leader. Without it, you're paddling the canoe up the rapids — lots of effort and little movement.

One way of establishing trust is through genuine dialogue. I pride myself on running meetings and facilitations in an organized way — honoring the commitments of time and work that individuals bring into the meetings. As a school principal, I often had the occasion to work with a staff in settings that called for high trust — it's the kind of trust that is earned through honest dealing and transparency when things are tough. In a school that may look like dealing honestly with student data, grappling with issues that create inequity, mediating conflicts between staff members fairly, or navigating relationships and communication between parents, teachers, and students.

Trust is earned over time and can be lost in an instant. Often, the fractured relationships I encountered between staff would be a result of broken trust. Someone said they were going to do something and didn't deliver, someone was disingenuous, or hidden agendas were at play.

People know when a leader is honest and real with them and genuinely tries to problem solve with them. Trust matters. The artful leader engages in high trust activities and when he fumbles, is honest and upfront about it, apologizes, and fixes it. Trust is often invisible when it is present, but its absence pollutes every decision and action in a thousand ways.

Trust, much like light, is essential for healthy, growing organizations. Without both, they become stunted and lost in the darkness.

chapter twenty-six

BETTER ANGELS

On March 4, 1861, President Lincoln delivered his first Inaugural Address:

> Though passion may have strained, it must not break our bonds of affection. The mystic chords of memory, stretching from every battle-field and patriot grave to every living heart and hearthstone, all over this broad land, will yet swell the chorus of the Union, when again touched, as surely they will be, by the better angels of our nature.

Lincoln, on the eve of civil war, urged us to summon the more noble parts of ourselves. You know those virtues, those that are the hardest to summon when they are the most important —such as kindness, humility, and service. While his stakes, there on the cusp of civil war, were much more profound than ours might be when we are launching a new initiative or resolving a conflict, nonetheless contain a kernel of truth there that is just as relevant in the daily conduct of your leadership and mine. It has much to do with the wisdom and character necessary to model compassionate, ethical practice even when it is the hardest to do.

Leaders, the good ones anyway, find their way through a host of daily occurrences that confront them by training, experience, and instinct. Living your values, guided by your own better angels, is an idea worth investing in. Trust me, your leadership will be better for it.

A BIT OF GRACE

We all have teachers along the way. My earliest teacher of this principle of leaning in towards grace was my mother. Now, I know, it is easy to see our mothers in a rarified light, one that emerges from the purity of their very special kind of love. I remember some years ago hearing Whoopi Goldberg speaking about her mother's death and how there were no sad goodbyes and she was at peace...except for one thing. She said that shortly after her mother's death she realized that no one would ever love her like that again, that she would never again put that same "sparkle" in anyone else's eye. Her words stuck with me. A mother's love is like that. Boundless and free. Mine was, anyway.

My mother, Gail, and she was a remarkable human being. I say was because she passed away a few months ago so the meaning of her life, and of its absence, is still fresh with me. I do not have the ability to share the things with you that are here about leadership grounded in humility, compassion, and grace, without acknowledging that where I first learned about those things was from my mother.

I was the first in my family to go to college. Each semester, I was aware of the struggle that she had to raise the tuition and fees for one more semester. I also went keenly aware of her pride in seeing me walk a path that she had never had the opportunity to walk, limited as she was by the times in which she lived, the economic realities of her life, and the responsibilities of a family. My mother was a school secretary. She worked hard and deeply valued the education she was never able to attain herself. It was a torch that I was to carry for us both.

It was a day of great celebration when I earned that first degree. I would go on to earn three more, each obtained while I was simultaneously working fulltime. Like my mother, I came to deeply value education and learning. In time, I would find my tribe in academia. The play of language, the study of literature and history, the analysis of research ever opening new doors to me — all of it drew me, like a moth to flame.

But before I even began to contemplate becoming a leader, I had learned much about empathy and compassion. My mother cared genuinely about everyone that she met in a way that I have rarely seen elsewhere in my life. Where others saw difference, she saw commonality. Where others found reason to judge, she counseled compassion and understanding. Many were the days that I remember being in the car with her or at bedtime, talking about how other's felt, how patience and understanding went a long way even when you were wronged, and the wisdom of not being too quick to judge others. "There but for the grace of God...," she would say. She was just a really good person, down to the core of her. One of the best. And I was privileged to be her son.

My mother never begrudged others for what she didn't have herself but was genuinely happy in their good fortune. She was a person who knew the value of so many things by their absence in her life, not their presence. Better angels, indeed.

One of the last lessons that she would teach me was importance of making your time count for something more. A few years ago, slowly at first, and then more suddenly, my mother's world began to shrink. She was losing her memory, the most cruel hand that fate could deal to a woman who found such deep meaning in the moments of her life and was grateful for each one.

It began simply with just repeating things, then forgetting them altogether. At first, it was inconsequential things, turning into increasingly important ones as time went on. Early in the decline of her memory, she would use skills such as writing in a journal to remember what happened each day. Before long, those strategies failed her, too. My mother began to set the table every day at her home, putting out plates, cups, utensils, and whatever she could find in her fridge. She was ready and waiting in case she had forgotten that it was a special day for someone or that there were young people coming from her church. When memory was gone, what remained was the love, generosity, and service that were in her very bones.

A year before her death, she moved into a memory care facility. Her rich and vibrant world had suddenly become quite small. Her self-proclaimed nickname had been "Ramblin' Rose" as she loved to always be on the go, always said yes to a trip or new adventure, and didn't like to waste a minute that was given her. She held every one precious, like so many fireflies in a mason jar.

Now, though, her world had suddenly became a small, eight by ten-foot room. The richness and beauty of the world she had known now was lost to her. Her log cabin, the quilts that her grandmother had made, handmade gifts of love from her children and grandchildren, family photos — all items whose voices were now silenced.

From the time that my sister and I were children, our family Christmas tree began transforming into an odd assemblage of objects — toy cars, felt figures, a cane here, a bird there. The tree was filled to the very limb and there was not a glass ball on it. From the time that we were children, we would gather each Christmas season and talk about what we were thankful for that year. A birth, a celebration of the life of someone who had passed, a graduation here, a marriage there. It was a tree of gratitude as it evolved over the many years of her life, it was a symbol of her sense of gratitude and grace.

I tell her story because it is one of grace, of better angels. If you are a leader, or aspire to be one, lead in ways that make a difference. Lead with humility, grace, and compassion. There is too much hatred and smallness in the world already. Don't add to it. Be led by your own better angels. They will serve you well in the difficult daily decisions that every leader has to make, just as they did President Lincoln when faced with inspiring a nation to come together even under the ravages of Civil War.

RUTHLESS

I once worked with the funny, wise woman by the name of Ruth. Ruth was retired but had agreed to come back to work. She had a keen sense of humor and was smart and creative. Ruth was a runner who did marathons around the world. In addition to her home in California, she owned a geodesic dome in Michigan. But if you knew Ruth, you would say, "Of course she does."

Ruth would leave to return to retirement now and then, only to come back when I called and told her we needed her and we just couldn't be "Ruth-less" anymore. She would laugh and say, "Okay, here I come!" She was a hoot, and a wise leader.

Ruth had frequently travelled to Hawaii. On one occasion I was planning what would be one of the last trips my mother and I would take. I was debating taking my mother to Hawaii. It would be a big trip, flying her from North Carolina to San Francisco, where I lived, and then on to

Hawaii. It would be expensive and would require a lot of time away from work. I had very nearly talked myself out of it when Ruth told me with great conviction, "Take your mother on the trip. What I wouldn't give," she said, "to have the chance to take my mother there one more time."

I took her advice. It was a trip filled with memories that will ever be burned into my mind. Those days, too, were some of the last ones my mother would remember. She would smile when she spoke of it. I am grateful for the grace of Ruth in reminding me how moments are to be seized, and not taken for granted.

Leading in this way, grounded in compassion and grace, establishes the kind of relationships and communication that stand you in good stead when true tests that will come to you as a leader. And come they will. Mine have been in the form of seemingly impossible, deep-seated challenges to overcome in ensuring that all students succeed. They also have come in those days when trusted colleagues and even mentors fail you when the chips are down.

Trust your better angels, particularly in those times when you are tested. Annie Dillard, one of my favorite authors, wrote that "I had been my whole life a bell, and never knew it until at that moment I was lifted and struck." Be ready when it is your time to ring!

Hold on to joy and meaning. Do work that matters. Be courageous and bold and compassionate as a leader. Make a difference and make things better for your having been here. Whenever you can, cease being Ruthless — and listen to those better angels — they won't steer you wrong.

chapter twenty-seven

LIVE OUT LOUD

S o, there was this jacket. I saw in a store over a couple of months, glinting from its rack beside the sales counter — a shining star in a field of ordinary.

The jacket was made of silver sequined material. I smiled when I saw it, but I told myself, "I could never. It is too much. It is too young, too loud, and, well, just too much!" But then, an adventurous friend convinced me to try it on while we were shopping together. Not only did it fit perfectly, he loved it. So, glancing at myself in the three-way mirror one last time, I kind of did too! So I splurged and bought the damn thing.

I hung my new oh-so-shiny jacket on the back of my bedroom door. It made me smile each morning as it winked at me. I had decided to give it a whirl on an upcoming trip to Vegas to see a concert. When I wore it, the comments started on the elevator ride down to the lobby to meet my sister...and they didn't stop! My sister and I started counting somewhere after the fifth or sixth compliment and stopped after we passed thirty! All over a jacket that very nearly didn't buy.

"That's the best jacket in town!"

"It's amazing!"

"Can I touch it?"

Absolute strangers would come up and comment, some gently touching it as if it were some rare species of sequined bird.

Something clicked in my consciousness — living (and even dressing) small and ordinary may make you blend in, but it will never make you stand out. The limits of my future as a fashion icon notwithstanding, living large, daring boldly, and making your ticket count are lessons the wise leader holds close.

If I have come to know one thing about life and leadership, it is this — live (and lead) big. Being meek, dissembling, or compromising your dreams doesn't get you anywhere. Live big. Take big chances. If you fall, fall on your ass spectacularly.

Make your ticket count for something. You only get one.

Leadership is a daunting undertaking. Done well, it is damned hard work. Don't do it for incremental gain or minimalistic goals. Dare boldly.

In leadership, as in jacket selection, I've come to believe that if you are going to go down, do so boldly. Take a stand for something that matters. We have enough dissembling compromise in our public policy and leadership. The type of bold leadership (and living) that we are talking about isn't without risk, political or otherwise. Yes, sometimes you will fall short, but you will do so daring greatly.

ONE FOR THE ROAD

So, whenever life hands you the opportunity to make a splash, do it. Make it the biggest damned cannonball into the pool they've ever seen. Live large.

And, just for good measure, here are a few more life lessons I've learned. Feel free to note them down somewhere. You're going to need them one day:

I've learned that you can pretty reliably count on kids and old people to tell you the truth about how much you weigh, how you look today, and what they really think about the food you prepared. A corollary to this lesson is: the truth hurts. So, there's that.

I've learned that when someone has screwed up, a little grace and compassion go a long way, even when you'd much rather dance in circles, waving your arms over your head and chanting "Told you so! Told you so!" Yeh, don't do that.

I've learned that there are three things that you can pretty much rely on when all else is iffy — that the car will stop making that funny noise when you get to the mechanic, the Christmas lights will be hopelessly tangled even though you rolled them neatly last year, and that the guy with the raging cold and the lady with the unhappy baby will vie for the seat beside you on the plane, bus, or train.

I've also learned that compassion isn't earned, and only really counts when extended to those who really have no reason to deserve it at all and likely won't return it.

I've learned that good leaders know when to abandon the ship of a bad idea and when to stay the course through the storms. I've learned that bad leaders pretty much consistently confuse these two things.

I've learned that people are drawn to the best leaders not because of their positions of power, but in spite of them.

I've learned that it is a law of physics that there are, in fact, invisible things on sidewalks that will trip you when the maximum number of people are around to see. I've learned that no matter how quickly you recover, toss your hair with a frothy laugh, and hurry on your way as if you are late to receive your Nobel Prize — everyone knows that you just tripped over the invisible thing.

I've learned that living life with an attitude of relentless grace is its own reward.

I've learned that people sometimes disappoint you, even when it matters most, but believe in the goodness of people anyway.

I've learned that, as art goes, a stroll through a random art gallery makes it pretty darned clear that it isn't the subject that matters — the perfect apple, shiny bowl of fruit, or multi-hued sunset — but how the thing is perceived that makes all of the difference. Trust your own vision, especially when it seems at odds with everyone else's.

Oh — and I've learned you should buy the damned jacket.

chapter twenty-eight

FUTURE FRUITS

A uthor Stewart Brand recounts a story he was told by English anthropologist Gregory Bateson of New College in Oxford that had been passed along to him. New College's name is a bit misleading as it was established in the fourteenth century. The college had an exquisite dining hall whose ceiling was spanned by massive oak beams.

The story went something like this. Some centuries ago, an entomologist climbed up to check the beams and, as he poked at them with an instrument, they crumbled to dust, devoured over the years by beetles.

This state of affairs caused the college council no end of consternation. These massive beams were broad and some forty-odd feet long and seemingly irreplaceable. But one fellow offered up that there might be some suitable trees on the college's lands. At least it was worth looking into. Contacting the college forester, they inquired on the off chance that there were sufficiently massive oaks on the grounds.

"Well," he is reported to have replied, "we were wondering when you would come for them." As it happened, when the college had been founded centuries before, a grove of oaks had been planted for this very purpose. The foresters of the time knew that all oak beams eventually succumb to beetles. Over the next 500 years, each forester passed on the instructions to his successor not to touch those trees, as they were for the college hall. Those foresters had known, centuries before, that those massive beams would eventually go to beetle and there would be a need to replace them. It was their job to nurture those seedlings that would grow to be massive oaks as they would be needed long after they were gone.

Our best and truest work addresses the needs of the moment, but also has an eye to what came before and what lies ahead. A few years ago, I conducted an internship with two students at a newly formed charter school in East Palo Alto, California. I had volunteered to mentor some students on a project related to the arts. Francisco and Mia were ninth graders at the school.

They had travelled different paths to get to this new charter school. Mia was a quiet student who didn't seem to have a lot to say or very strong opinions, but she was interested in doing this internship as she loved music. Francisco was a charismatic young man with a big personality, but a troubled academic history marked by learning challenges. Both, I was to learn, were quite remarkable young people.

Upon our first meeting, we talked about some possible work that we might do together over the course of the year. An option I presented to them was studying the legacy of Grace McCann Morley, the first director of the San Francisco Museum of Modern Art. Beginning in the 1930s, Grace was one of the first female directors of a major art museum in the country. I knew a bit about Grace and her legacy and was fascinated by her, but there was much still to uncover. Francisco and Mia were interested in learning more and so we set to work to understand the context in which we could understand Grace.

The students conducted some initial background study on populism and the long history and legacy of SFMOMA. They learned how this museum had brought modern art to the people as opposed to the more traditional model of the time, which involved museums featuring classical works for the elite. The students read about the political milieu of the 1940s in San Francisco and the conditions for women in the workforce during that era.

Deepening their inquiry, they began to explore documentary records and artifacts related to the life of service of this remarkable woman, Grace McCann Morley, who led the SFMOMA in the 1930s. She brought her vision of a different kind of museum, raised funds to build a collection, and oversaw the complex and arduous physical assembly of that collection. Her work was fueled by vision and perseverance. Its legacy extends to this day.

The year's work culminated in our spending a day together at the SFMOMA. A curator of the painting collection gave us a private tour and spoke to us about the works at the museum that were acquisitions of, or legacies to, Grace. After the tour, the curator sat down for an interview with the students. Both of these students were a bit like 9th graders everywhere — uncertain and suddenly shy when put on the spot; Mia particularly was soft-spoken and a bit timid.

Every bit the ninth grader, Francisco apologized for forgetting his notebook but nonetheless asked a couple of questions about the works of art that Grace had curated and her impact on the museum. Then Mia cleared her throat and spoke, quietly at first, and then quite literally finding her voice. It would not be the last time that this young woman would surprise me when called on to step up.

"We talked about how uncommon it was for a woman to be in this position of power in the '30s and '40s," she started strongly. "Has that changed today? Is it really different? What is it like for women to be in top leadership roles in museums in the 21st century?" There was a quiet in the room as the curator looked up from her notes. The conversation suddenly had shifted from a polite docent answering students' predictable questions to an honest and real conversation about gender politics in the museum business. Everyone turned to Mia, not expecting such a direct and insightful question from this slight and shy girl.

The curator looked at her squarely and then honestly told her that it is still difficult, and disturbingly uncommon, for women to achieve posts at the pinnacle of museum leadership in America's major museums. She spoke passionately about her own journey through the leadership of various museums and the realities of that journey and navigating her career while starting and raising a family.

For her part, Mia didn't nod and sit quietly, but probed deeper with follow-up questions like some intrepid veteran investigative reporter. She left with us all having a deeper and more nuanced understanding not only of Grace McCann Morley but also about gender equity and the social and gender dynamics of major American museums. It was a real moment, the kind that sticks with you, and one that none of us had expected or would soon forget. I think that Grace would have been proud of her. I know that I was.

This was not the only day that Mia or Francisco would remind me of the power of agency and empowerment in young people's lives. Later in the year, I invited them to speak at a countywide arts leadership breakfast. I had invited them, as a coda on the end of their project. They had come to talk with the assembled educators and community leaders about what they had learned about Grace and what meaning that had found in that work in the context of their own lives in East Palo Alto, a community in which many residents live below the poverty line, though bordered by communities of great affluence.

The scene was at a large, modern meeting facility. A student string quartet played as a stream of community and educational leaders entered.

Early in the agenda, after a series of welcomes, Francisco and Mia made their comments. Both of these students enraptured the crowd, telling them of the power of the arts in their lives and how they resonated and connected with the life of Grace McCann Morley. Mia spoke of challenges she had weathered in her life and how music had been her refuge and salvation. Both had the audience spellbound and revealed not only the power of the arts, but of taking a stand, being genuine, and daring boldly. We all took a lesson from these young people.

Francisco and Mia's stories model the power of inquiry and reflection. The leader that they studied was herself a model of bold vision, courage, and the potential to change the trajectory of systems that impact lives. The cherry on the particular sundae was when Francisco and Mia contacted me later that year as they were curating a student photo exhibition about life in their inner-city community — a fitting nod to the legacy of Grace McCann Morley.

There is a quote of uncertain origins. Some posit its origin is Greek, while others suggest its derivation is more modern. The quote posits that the meaning of life is to plant trees in whose shade you will never sit. I think that's right. For most leaders, much of the work you will do will likely bear fruit long after you are gone.

Thus, much like the foresters at New College, the artful leader has a long view. She knows that the work she does today will pay dividends that she may never see. This is a long view that asks all of us to have a somewhat blind faith in those that will follow, a steady commitment to our True North, and confidence that those who follow will have the wisdom to build upon what was planted by those who came before.

The artful leader leaves a legacy he or she may never get to enjoy. Yet that legacy will resonate for ages.

chapter twenty-nine

DON'T WASTE YOUR TICKET

It was an exquisite day. I had just arrived in Puerto Vallarta, my favorite spot for rest and relaxation. It was a perfect day — it was not too hot and there was the promise of a cold margarita in my immediate future, followed by an evening outing on friend's yacht. Mostly, though, it was a brief respite from the mounting pressures of the campaign trail.

The yacht was a true work of art: polished inlaid wood, gleaming white exteriors, and a lovely and peaceful lounge area with a bar. Dinner was served on the aft deck — the stories, laughter, and wine were flowing freely. The evening sky had darkened; even the glittering lights from the coastline were fading into the distance.

A member of the crew whispered in the ear of one of our hosts, and he tapped his fork on his glass to get our attention.

"Sometimes in the tropics," he said, "plankton is bioluminescent and puts on quite a spectacular show. Come join me on the stern."

We paused our dining and conversing, curious about what we were going to see, and walked with him to the stern of the deck. We peered over the edge of the boat into the inky darkness of the Pacific, and I have never forgotten what I saw there.

Swimming alongside the boat, were the glowing outlines of dolphins cutting through the bioluminescent plankton. It was something I didn't fully understand, and, quite literally, it took my breath away. This magical moment of the glowing images of dolphins in shimmering greens and blues diving and leaping alongside the boat as it cut its way through the inky night took my breath away. The memory of that evening still does.

Sometimes in life, when stressors pile up and critics pile on, it is good to remember that there is wonder out there. That night was one in which that lesson was seared into my consciousness. It occurred at a moment when I was deep into the impossible hours and schedule of running a political campaign while simultaneously working a demanding, full-time job. I had the sudden realization that the stress, stakes, and difficulty of the choices before me were merely situational constructs that I had chosen. I had not known or even considered that somewhere in the world, there were *glowing dolphins* swimming through pitch black water. Somehow, that put everything else into perspective.

In the cosmic game of life, glowing dolphins always win. What else had I missed by limiting my field of vision? What other possibilities were out there around the next corner?

If there is a message for both life and leadership that I can leave with you, it is this: Life is damned short. Make yours count.

I know you've heard it before. It is a dusty truism that we remember only at key junctures such as when a loved one dies or when we have our own run-in with danger. I didn't used to think about that much back when time passing slowly seemed a nuisance. When I was a teenager waiting to be old enough to drive, when I a harried student thinking I would never get through my dissertation and get to the end, I always thought that once those things happened, it would all be sweet. I still remember my grandmother standing in her kitchen and reminding me to enjoy each moment: "You will want these days back one day," she would say. "Don't wish them away."

It was good advice. Really.

Now, don't get me wrong, I spend way too many hours working, commuting, and worrying about organizational problems and issues, many of which are truthfully quite insignificant in the grander scheme of things. But I am also keenly aware that this movie we call life has a limited run and what you make of your time matters.

I bet you've known people who were waiting for the next thing to happen to be happy — the next job, the raise, the lottery, or the knight in shining armor riding over yon hill. To them I say, let that go and find joy in your now. If those things happen, you can rock out and enjoy them when they do, but too many people live lives of sullen despair feeling like victims of their lives...waiting for some elusive thing to happen. The trick is finding joy even when life deals you a crappy hand.

My grandmother was an amazing human-being. She loved the beach. I remember walking with her on the beach as a young child, a plastic pail and shovel in my hands. She used to tell me that when I was little, I would whimper just a little when the waves would hit my feet, but I never complained and just kept walking. I think that is kind of how I have tried to live my life. Always one foot in front of the other, even when the cold waves hit my feet.

It is when we embrace the joy, and even the pain, of life that we truly become who we are capable of being. And the best leaders — those who change things, create new possibilities, and build something that didn't exist before — do so from a deep place of knowing, centeredness, and connection.

If all you do as a leader is implement policies, keep the machine chugging along, and minimize risk, then you never really know what you were capable of. And, who knows, it could have been something truly amazing.

A FINAL WORD

I've known people who exemplify that old chestnut about glasses half empty or full. I've known those who have argued passionately on both sides of that debate. I try to live my life in a space of gratitude and gracefulness. There are days when that kind of grace is hard to summon: when someone acts in a rude or hurtful way, when someone takes advantage or is manipulative, when I give something my all and fall short. Yes, there are some days when it's hard to summon that grace.

I have a good friend named Cole. He is a musician, composer, performer, and the kind of friend who will always tell you the truth, whether you want to hear it or not. I like that about him.

Cole's grandmother was a San Francisco native and a lifelong Giants fan. She never missed an opening game in her long and colorful life. She was a true, blue Giants fan through and through. A few years ago, his grandmother died. She had left specific instructions for her funeral.

Now, the priests gave them some flack as they planned the service, but they compromised, in the end. As her casket was carried from the service and hit the doors of the church, a rousing chorus of "Take Me Out to the Ballgame" erupted spontaneously from those gathered, the mixture of joy in her life and sorrow in her loss inextricably woven together in the melodies. There was not a dry eye as they sang, at the top of their lungs, her favorite song.

But the old bird had one more trick up her sleeve. As her casket arrived at the gravesite, the melody of "I Left My Heart in San Francisco" wafted through the air. It was her pre-arranged parting gift to them all. Moments like put everything in perspective — all of those things that had seemed so important suddenly small beans in our grand cosmic opera.

It reminded me of my own father's funeral. A revered fire station Captain, uniformed firefighters carried his casket to a black-draped firetruck to be transported to the gravesite where a silver bell was rung for him. As its tone reverberated through the cold October air, the fire fighters' radios all sparked to life as the final dispatch for my dad was issued over the airwaves. It is a moment seared into my memory, his passion and life's work coming together in his final sendoff.

There is a special kind of passion that sustains us, even to the end. It is a thing of beauty. Life is made up of small moments of such passion, jagged bits of tile fitted together to form a mural of a life — vivid and lovely and terrible and divine. We don't get to shape all of that mural, but now and then we get to shape some of it through radical acts of kindness, compassion, and artfulness.

I hope that my leadership, and yours, will inspire people to live and lead with this kind of passion and sense of hope and promise.

So lead. Lead boldly and bravely. Lead with humility and grace. You don't have to have all of the answers. Just keep asking the right questions and lead with a bent towards empathy, humanity, and light and you will make a difference.

And that will make it all worthwhile.

ACKNOWLEDGEMENTS

Writing a book is a journey. Like any good journey, it doesn't hurt to have some awesome people along for the ride with you.

And I did.

I'd like to thank my mother from whom I inherited my penchant for self-reflection and my love of coffee. Both of these things were essential to this book coming to fruition.

My mom passed away recently, but I know she would have taken a shine to this book. I know so because when we cleared out her home, I found mementos of just about everything I've ever done since I was a kid: kindergarten etchings on foil, a newspaper clipping from a poetry contest I won as a teenager, birthday cards, tickets from trips we took, a rockin' pair of red velvet overalls from my first birthday and, yes, even my doctoral dissertation. It was all there, treasured and lovingly preserved. I'm crazy lucky to have been that special to somebody. I never took that for granted.

And the coffee thing, too.

I'd also like to thank Anne Lamott. Just to be clear, I don't know Anne Lamott. So, hi Anne, I'm Gary. Nevertheless, her seminal book, *Bird by*

Bird, inspired me to write something simple and true. I told my story, as best I could, the way I lived it and, thanks to Anne, didn't worry about the shitty first draft. She reminded me that I am, in her words, "lucky to be one of those people who wishes to build sand castles with words." I always liked sand castles.

And words.

Much of what I know is a consequence of bumps and bruises that I earned along the way. I am deeply grateful to those who have mentored me, challenged me, and believed in my journey... as well as those from whom I earned those bumps and bruises as they have been a source of deeper empathy and understanding. Ok, so, in all honesty, most days I'm way more grateful to the former group. To the latter crew, some of you were real assholes. Still, there is something there about grains of sand, oysters, and pearls that I could ruminate on. But still. Yeh.

I am immensely grateful those good souls who helped in the writing, rethinking, revising, and eventual finishing of this book. They offered me their unvarnished feedback and I am in their debt. These are Dr. Jean Holbrook, Rebecca Vyduna, Byron Ballard, Steve Redell, and Susan Alvaro, among others.

I will be forever grateful to those whose stories are included here, offered as I experienced them. Some are acknowledged by name, some by pseudonym, and some without names — but you know who you are. I owe you each a debt of gratitude which I try, each day, to pay forward in my leadership.

Thanks to those who helped me across the finish line; editor, June Saunders, the designers, artists, and all of the wise and artful guides who lit the path.

A special thanks, too, to my friend Avi Juni from whom I learned a lot about being an artist as well as a person. Thanks to him, too, for his way cool concept cover art.

Lastly, I tip my proverbial hat to my dear friend Cheryl, who is gone now. She would have dug this. Mostly for the funny bits. Well, maybe the heartfelt bits too. Mostly she would have liked it because it is about how to leave the world a better place for having been here. Just like she did.

Cheryl, I hope I got it right (the book, and the rest, too).

And lastly, to you, my erstwhile reader, thank you for sitting a spell with me. I hope you found a kernel of something in here to mull over and give a whirl around the block that leaves your own corner of the world a little better, a little more artful, and just a little kinder.

We need more of that.

A FINAL WORD

Before you go, don't forget to claim your special parting gift (after all, a little swag makes every party better!)

Download your free *The Art of Everything Workbook.*

This short guide will help you implement the elements of the Framework for Artful Leadership and provide some suggestions to jump start your own reflection on the core guideposts of artful leadership.

Download your free workbook at www.garywaddell.org/bonus

(And while you're there, be sure to subscribe for additional bonus content and updates!)

To learn more, connect with the author, or inquire about speaking engagements, visit www.garywaddell.org/art or email artofeverything@ garywaddell.org.

FURTHER READING

The following list, which includes some sources referenced in this book, also contains recommendations for further reading on the principles of artful leadership.

Brand, Stewart. *How buildings learn: What happens after they're built.* New York: Penguin Books. 1995.

Brown, Tim. *Change by design: How design thinking transforms organizations and inspires innovation.* New York: Harper Collins. 2009.

Frankl, Viktor. *Man's search for meaning.* Boston, MA: Beacon Press. 1984.

Gaiman, Neil. *Make good art.* New York: William Morrow. 2013.

Gilbert, Elizabeth. *Big magic: Creative living beyond fear.* New York: Penguin Publishing. 2015.

Kinsey, Bernard and Kinsey, Shirley. *The Kinsey collection: Shared treasures of Bernard and Shirley Kinsey.* California: The Bernard and Shirley Kinsey Foundation. 2009.

Kirk, Kara. *Grace McCann Morley and the modern museum.* SFMOMA.org. https://www.sfmoma.org/essay/grace-mccann-morley-and-modern-museum/. 2017.

Kuhn, Thomas. *The structure of scientific revolutions.* Chicago: University of Chicago Press. 1996.

Lamott, Anne. *Bird by bird: Some instructions on writing and life.* New York: Anchor. 2007.

Meier, Deborah. The Power of Their Ideas: Lessons for America from a Small School in Harlem. Boston: Beacon Press. 1995.

Sklar, Marty. *Dream it! Do it!: My half-century creating Disney's magic kingdoms.* United States: Disney Editions. 2013.

Speier, Jackie. *Undaunted: Surviving Jonestown, summoning courage, and fighting back.* United States: Little A. 2018.

Wheatley, Meg. *Leadership and the new science: Discovering order in a chaotic world.* California: Berrett-Koehler Publishers. 2006.

Made in the USA
Monee, IL
28 November 2020